Flawed Like Me

By Darren Brown

Library of Congress Control Number: 2020909365

ISBN: 978-1-7923-3997-4

Printed in the United States by Morris Publishing®
3212 East Highway 30
Kearney, NE 68847
1-800-650-7888

Table of Content:

Preface

There is any number of clichés for different changes and phases that life presents:

- If God can use a donkey, He can certainly use you (or me).
- God can put together the pieces of your broken life.
- If you make one step, God will make two.
- When life gives you lemons, make lemonade.
- There's always more than one way to skin a cat (not literally of course).
- Life is like a rollercoaster; enjoy the ride.
- Etc. etc. etc....

This book started as a Sunday school project and after talking to a few people about the outline it quickly became apparent that it should be a book. Often we read, or listen to stories about various bible characters and walk away with a variety of feelings. Feelings ranging from my life is a mess and God would never use me like that; to that is awesome, I want to be just like that. The purpose of this book is to prayerfully inspire someone to grow past, or persevere through what they may consider the biggest mistake/failure of their life.

We spend a lot of time marveling over the powerful way in which God used different individuals in the bible, but most of us, if not nearly all of us never consider their humanity.

Introduction

In today's society, most, if not all young people are looking for a role model. For some, it's their favorite athlete; some a celebrity; others a successful businessperson. However, looking for someone to pattern one's life after is not new to this generation. There was a time most people wanted to emulate a parent, a successful relative, or maybe even a superhero, for those that dared to dream of being something other than merely human. There is something built into the basic fabric of who or what we are as a species, that compels us to do better; regardless of what that better may be. We tend to find something that we are passionate about; seek out someone currently doing it, or has done it, and improve upon it. Not only to make it better but to make it our own.

More often than not, it was a quiet aspiration. In essence, admiring qualities in other people from a distance; so to speak. Then in 1992, Gatorade, cashed in on a brilliant ad campaign and that silent aspiration became very vocal. Suddenly people were verbalizing, "I wanna be like Mike!" Of course, you can replace "Mike" with whomever it is you would like to emulate, but you get the point. For me, I had two people and neither one was famous to anyone but me....

But what happens when your role model falls from grace? How does it affect you when you find out that this person has a pretty bad character flaw? Do you get angry? Do you swear never to follow that person ever again? Do you feel a sense of betrayal? Do you "blow it off" and maintain focus on the good traits that you admired in that person to begin with? Does your reaction change when that person is someone you know personally? My first role model was my father. As a little boy growing up, he was larger than life. He was a strict disciplinarian, but he was very engaging with us and our friends. So much so, he would even participate in some of our games, all of our races, and always had an encouraging word. He had the respect of everyone in town, which didn't always work out so well for me (if you know what I mean). Then one day, I found out, there was no Santa Claus, the Easter bunny didn't lay eggs, and the tooth fairy didn't pay you for losing a tooth. Now imagine what it felt like to a child that got spanked every time he/she was caught in a lie. The devastation of finding out that your parents are not only liars, but they are hypocrites too.

Fortunately, such an experience doesn't cause irreparable damage to the vast majority of people. They become productive citizens that pass along that deception to their children. Everyone reacts to disappointments in life differently. Most are able to take the good, toss out the bad, and use it as a learning experience to grow. For some, it's a temporary jolt to their reality, and they quickly re-evaluate things and keep it moving. Then there are the select few that it thoroughly devastates; they become disenfranchised and give up on their dreams. With Christian role models, it's different. We get to see that person after they've been touched by God. We stand in awe of the miraculous. We dance and shout about what God does through them. So much so, that we overlook their humanity. Some people are so awe-struck, that they look at where they are in life and feel discouraged because they figure their lives are a total wreck and God won't use them. It's almost as if we completely forget that Christian role models are flesh and blood like we are: subject to the same issues that we face today, and zoom in on the awe-inspiring.

He walked on water: how cool would that be? Never mind

the fact, his loss of focus caused him to sink.

He was the greatest preacher of his time; I mean how many preachers do you know saved over 100,000 people with a seven-word message? Never mind, his attitude was so poor he nearly caused the death of innocent sailors.

The examples are right in front of us to examine. Focusing on their humanity allows us to see that God can, and will use us because they were FLAWED Like Me.

Jacob: Change my Name; Change my Character

Yeah, I know what you're thinking. You see my name and the first thing that comes to mind for most of you is: there goes that trickster. A lot of you even think my name means trickster or supplanter, but you would be wrong. So, don't confuse my name with my actions. Jacob, in reality, means he who follows; or if you translate the original root word, it means heel grabber.

There is also another lesson to be learned at the beginning of my story. Parents, be very careful when you choose favorites between your children, things might not turn out the way you expect. In this case, they worked out pretty well, in a roundabout sort of way. However, that's a discussion for another time.

My story started in turmoil with a problematic pregnancy for my mother Rebekah and continued in turmoil through most of my adult life. My mother wasn't able to have children until she prayed to the Lord. Hindsight being 20/20, I'll bet she wished, she had been a bit more specific with her prayer. God answered her prayer with twin boys. Not just any twin boys, we were polar opposites. We tussled and contended with each other constantly in the womb. So much so, it troubled our mother to the point that she sought God for an answer to the turmoil going on inside her. He answered: "Two nations are in your womb. The two will be separated; one people will be stronger than the other, and the older will serve the younger."

According to the time of life, mother gave birth to my brother Esau first, and even at birth, we were still at it. Well maybe not we, it was more so me. I had ahold of my brother's heel as if I was trying to pull him back into the womb so I could be first. As we grew up, Esau became a skillful hunter and therefore, he was dad's favorite. I was more of a quiet homebody type, and mother's favorite. One day I was making some stew and Esau came in from the field. He was starving, having caught nothing all day, and he asked for some stew. I replied, "I'll give you some stew for your birthright", and Esau said, "I'm about to die, what good is a birthright going to do me?" As I was about to hand Esau a bowl of stew I said, "Swear to me first." So, Esau swore and sold me the birthright.

Father has gotten old and has gone blind. I'm feeling like he may die soon. Mother came to me after she overheard a conversation between father and Esau. She said, "I overheard your father say to your brother 'Bring me some game and prepare me a tasty dish to eat. After that I will bless you in the presence of the LORD before I die.' Now, my son, listen to me and do exactly what I tell you. Go out to the flock and bring me two choice young goats, so that I can make a tasty dish for your father. Then take it to your father to eat, so that he may bless you before he dies." I guess now you see who the real trickster is. Don't get me wrong, I fully understand why she was doing it. Mother had told me about the prophecy she had received when she was pregnant, but I'm sure God would have fulfilled His prophecy without our help. I said, "Mother, you're forgetting one very important detail. Esau is hairy and my skin is smooth. What if father touches me? I would be revealed to him as a deceiver, and I would bring a curse upon myself rather than a blessing." She replied, "Just do exactly what I say and everything will be just fine. I have it all under control." I did as I was told and watched my mother do her thing. She prepared the goat just the way father liked it. Then she got some of Esau's clothes and I put them on. Last but not least, she put the skin of the young goats on my hands and neck.

I entered into my father's tent with his food and said, "My

father, here I am!" He answered. "Which one are you, my son?" "I am Esau, your firstborn. I have done as you asked. Please sit up and eat some of my game, after which you may bless me." Isaac asked, "How did you find it so quickly, my son?" "Because the LORD your God brought it to me," I replied. I could tell by the look on his face that he wasn't convinced I was Esau. Then he asked me to come closer, so he could touch me and tell who I truly was. I moved close to him and he touched me. He said, "The voice is the voice of Jacob, but the hands, are the hands of Esau." He let my hands go; still not completely sure it was Esau, he asked one last time, "Are you truly my son Esau?" I replied, "I am." Then I gave him his food and some wine. After he finished, he said, "Come close so I can kiss you. I did so, and when Isaac smelled the clothing, he blessed me and said: "Ah, the smell of my son is like the smell of a field that the LORD has blessed. May God give to you the dew of heaven and the richness of the earth, and an abundance of grain and new wine. May peoples serve you and nations bow down to you. May you be the master of your brothers, and may the sons of your mother bow down to you. May those who curse you be cursed, and those who bless you be blessed." After that, I left my father's presence and just in the nick of time. Esau was returning from his hunt.

Not long after Esau returned, mother sent for me. When I reached her, she was in a panic and said, "Your brother is furious at what you have done, and wants to kill you. Go to Haran, and stay with my brother Laban. Stay there a few days until your brother's anger subsides and he no longer wants to kill you. When he has forgotten what you have done, I will send for you. I can't bear to lose both of you in one day. I'm thinking, what I have done? I wouldn't even be in this situation if you hadn't put me up to this. It is just as much your fault as it is mine. Later that day, still displeased with my deception, father called me to his tent and blessed me, saying, "Do not take a wife from the Canaanite women," "Go at once to Paddan-aram, to the house of your mother's father Bethuel, and take a wife from among the daughters of Laban. May God Almighty bless you and make you fruitful and multiply you, so that you may become a great people. May He give the blessing of Abraham to you and your descendants, so that you may possess the land where you dwell as a foreigner, the land God gave to Abraham."

On the way to Haran, I reached a certain place and spent the night there because the sun had set. I took a stone and put it under his head and laid down to sleep. I had a dream about a ladder that rested on the earth with its top reaching up to heaven, and God's angels were going up and down the ladder. At the top of the ladder, the LORD was standing and saying, "I am the LORD, the God of your father Abraham and the God of Isaac. I will give you and your descendants the land on which you now lie. Your descendants will be like the dust of the earth, and you will spread out to the west and east and north and south. All the families of the earth will be blessed through you and your children. I am with you, and I will watch over you wherever you go. I will bring you back to this land. I will not leave you until I have done what I have promised you." When I woke up, I said, "Surely the Lord was in the place, and I didn't know it. How awesome is this place! This is none other than the house of God; this is the gate of heaven!" Early the next morning, I took the stone that I had placed under my head and set it up as a pillar. I poured oil on it and called that place Bethel. Then I made a vow saying, "If God will be with me and watch over me on this journey, and if He will provide me with food to eat and clothes to wear, so that I may return safely to my father's house, then the LORD will be my God. All that You give me I will surely give You a tenth."

I continued my journey and came to a well. There were three flocks of sheep waiting to be watered, but a large stone covered the mouth of the well. When all the flocks had been gathered there, the shepherds rolled the stone away from the mouth of the well and watered the sheep. "My brothers, where are you from?" I asked. They answered, "We are from Haran." "Do you know Laban, grandson of Nahor?" I asked. "We know him, and here comes his daughter Rachel with his sheep." they replied. When she arrived at the well, I told her that I was Rebekah's son, a relative of her father, and she ran and told her father. When Laban heard the news, he ran out to meet me. He took me to his home, and I told him everything that had happened. Then Laban declared, "You are indeed my flesh and blood." I'm not quite sure how to take that statement. Would he have said the same thing if I had not told him about my predicament?

After I had been with him a month, Laban said to me, "Just because you are my relative; you should not work for nothing. Tell me what your wages should be." I answered, "I will work for you seven years for your younger daughter Rachel." Laban replied, "Better that I give her to you than to someone else." So, I worked seven years for Rachel, but it seemed like a few months because I loved her. At the end of my service, I said to Laban, "Give me my wife." Laban invited all the men of that place and prepared a feast. When evening came; Laban took his daughter Leah and gave her to me, and I slept with her. I know, all of you have wondered, how drunk was I, that I did not know the difference between Leah and Rachel. It seems that I was VERY drunk. In the morning, there was Leah next to me. I found Laban and asked, "What have you done to me? I worked for Rachel. Why have you deceived me?" Laban replied, "It is not our custom to give the younger daughter in marriage before the older. Finish this week's celebration, and I will give you Rachel for another seven years of work." It appears that deception is a family trait, and maybe I should have picked up on that fact earlier. You know, like when I first questioned his statement about being family. I guess turnabout is fair play. I deceived my father to get his blessing, and now I've been deceived and denied the one that I loved. I was furious, and I imagined this is how Esau must have felt. I agreed to his terms because I loved Rachel. At the end of the celebration he gave Rachel to me as my wife, and I worked for Laban another seven years.

The LORD saw that Leah was hated. He opened her womb, and Rachel was barren. Leah conceived and gave birth to a son, and she named him Reuben. She said, "The LORD has seen my affliction. Surely my husband will love me now." Again, she conceived and gave birth to a son and said, "Because the LORD has heard that I am hated", and she named him Simeon. For the third time, Leah conceived and gave birth to a son, and said, "Now, at last, my husband will become attached to me, because I have borne him three sons." So, he was named Levi. Once more, she conceived and gave birth to a son and said, "This time I will praise the LORD", and she named him Judah.

I found myself in an ironic situation: the woman that I did not desire, or particularly care for, has given me what all men desire most: sons. While the one that I desired the most, has given me nothing. Even worse, she came to me jealous and upset with Leah. She said, "Give me children, or I will die!" I replied angrily, "Am I God, who has withheld children from you?" Then she said, "Here is my maidservant Bilhah. Sleep with her, and she will bear children for me so that through her I too can build a family." Through all the contention and jealousy, I now have 11 sons and a daughter.

From Leah: Reuben- behold a son
        Simeon- to hear, listen
        Levi- accompany, joined to
        Judah- praise
        Issachar- there is a reward, my hire
        Zebulun- honor
        Dinah- avenged, judged and vindicated

From Bilhah: Dan- judge
           Naphtali- my struggle, my strife

From Zilpah Gad- fortunate, luck
           Asher- happy one

From Rachel: Joseph- he increases

Now I'm beginning to feel like it's time for me to take my
family and move on. So, I said to Laban, "Let me leave,
so I can go unto mine own place, and to my country. Give
me my wives and children, and I will go on my way. You
know how hard I have worked for you." Laban replied,
"I beg you, if I have found favor in your eyes, please stay.
I have learned by experience that the LORD has blessed
me for your sake. So, name your price, and I will pay it."
I said, "You had very little before I arrived, but now your
wealth has increased many times over. The LORD has
blessed you wherever I walk. When can I also provide
for my household? If you do this one thing for me, I will
continue shepherding and keeping your flock. Let me go
through your flocks and remove every speckled or spotted
sheep, every dark-colored lamb, and every spotted or
speckled goat. That will be my price." Laban agreed to
my terms and we stayed. That same day, Laban divided
the flock according to our agreement. I took mine and
Laban gave his to his sons. As time passed my flock grew
larger than Laban's, and his sons became jealous and
angry. I overheard them saying, "Jacob has taken away
all that belonged to our father and built all this wealth at
our father's expense." No matter what I do; it seems like
trouble always finds me. Then the LORD said to me, "Go
back to the land of your fathers and kindred, and I will be
with you." I called Rachel and Leah, and told them, "I can
see your father's attitude toward me has changed, but the
God of my father has been with me. You know that I have

served your father with all my strength; even though he has cheated me and changed my wages ten times. God has not allowed him to harm me." Rachel and Leah replied, "All the wealth that God has taken away from our father belongs to us and our children. So, do whatever God has told you." So, I packed up my family, and gathered the livestock, and left Haran. We crossed the Euphrates and headed for the hills of Gilead. We reached Mt. Gilead and Laban showed up with his brethren. Laban confronted me saying, "What have you done? You have deceived me and carried off my daughters like captives of war! Why did you run away secretly and deceive me, without even telling me? I would have sent you away with joy and singing, with tambourines and harps. You did not even let me kiss my daughters and grandchildren goodbye." Is this man serious? Of all the people, he is the last one to be talking about being deceived. He has lied and cheated at every turn. Then he has the audacity to say he would let me go, had I just said something. It appears that he had forgotten, I did say it was time for me to take my family and move away from him. He continued to say, "You left because you longed for your father's house, but you have done a foolish thing. Why have you stolen my gods? Now, I have the power to do you great harm to you, but last night the God of your father said to me, 'Be careful not to say or do anything to Jacob, either good or bad.'" I responded, "I was afraid. I thought you would take your daughters from me by force. As for your gods, if you find them with anyone here, he shall not live! In the presence of our relatives, look for yourself, and if you find anything of yours, take it back." Laban searched the camp and could not find the gods he was searching for. So, I got angry and argued with him, saying, "What is my crime? What sin of mine made you so hotly pursue after me? You have searched all my goods! Have you found anything that is yours? Put it here before our brothers and, and they may judge between us. I have been with you for twenty years now. Your sheep and goats have not miscarried, nor have I eaten the rams of your flock. I did not bring you anything torn by wild beasts. I bore the loss myself, and you have changed my wages ten times! If the God of my father, the God of Abraham and the One feared by Isaac, had not been with me, you would have sent me away empty-handed by now. However, God had seen my affliction and the toil of my hands, and last night He rendered judgment." We worked out our differences and sat down for a meal. The next morning Laban got up, kissed his grandchildren, blessed his daughter, and returned to his home.

As we continue on our journey to Canaan, I was met by the angels of God. I said to myself, "This is the camp of God", and I named that place Mahanaim. I sent messengers ahead to meet Esau in the land of Seir, the country of Edom. I told them, "You are to say to Esau, 'Your servant Jacob says: I have been staying with Laban until now. I have oxen, donkeys, flocks, menservants, and maidservants. I have sent this message to inform you, so that I may find favor in your sight.'" When the messengers returned, they said, "We went to your brother Esau; he is coming to meet you, and he has four hundred men with him." After I heard that, a VERY cold chill went down my spine. Esau still hates me and is coming to get his revenge. In great fear and distress, I divided my people into two camps, as well as the flocks and herds. I figure, if Esau attacked me, the others can escape. I calmed myself and prayed, "O God of my father Abraham, God of my father Isaac; LORD you told me, go back to your country and your family, and I will make you prosper. I am unworthy of all the kindness and faithfulness You have shown me. I came across the Jordan with little more than a staff, but now I have become two camps. Please deliver me from the hands of my brother Esau. I am afraid that he may come and attack me and my family. You said, 'I will surely make you prosper, and I will make your children like the sand of the sea, too numerous to count.'"

After that, I selected a gift for Esau, 200 female goats; 20 male goats; 200 ewes; 20 rams; 30 milk camels with their young; 40 cows; 10 bulls; 20 female donkeys, and 10 male donkeys. I gave them to my servants in separate herds and told them, "Go on ahead of me, and keep some distance between the herds." I told the one in the lead, "When my brother Esau meets you and asks, 'To whom do you belong, where are you going, and whose animals are these before you?' then you are to say, 'They belong to your servant Jacob. They are a gift, sent to my lord Esau, and behold, Jacob is behind us.'" I then told the second, the third, and all those following behind the herds: "When you meet Esau, you are to say the same thing to him, also say, 'Look, your servant Jacob is right behind us.'" For he thought, he would appease Esau with the gift that is going before me. After that, I can face him, and perhaps he will accept me." I sent them on and spent the night in the camp alone.

That night a man came and we wrestled until daybreak. When the man realized He could not overpower me; He struck my hip and the pain was excruciating. Yet I still held on to him for dear life. Then the man said, "Let Me go, for it is daybreak." I replied, "I will not let You go unless You bless me." He said, "What is your name?" "I replied, it's Jacob." Then he said, "Your name will no longer be Jacob, but Israel, because you have power with God and with men, and you have prevailed." I asked him, "What is Your name." "Why do you need to know My name?" he replied. Then He blessed me there, and I named that place Peniel, saying, "Indeed, I have seen God face to face, and my life was spared." After the man had blessed me and departed, I realized how much damage was done. My hip was dislocated and now I have a pronounced limp. So, I limped back across the stream to get my family and the rest of my possessions. We set out to meet my fate with Esau. Something is seriously bugging me. I devised a plan to appease my brother, which is contradictory to the promise I had from God, and the prayer that I prayed after finding out that he was coming with 400 men. Some habits, in fact, are hard to break. I guess it's time for me to actually trust God and see what happens.

I looked out and saw Esau with four hundred men in the distance. Well, maybe this might not be the best time to trust God. I don't know what I'm doing. Why would Esau bring 400 men with him if he wasn't planning to kill me? I don't want to risk losing my family. So, I divided the children among Leah, Rachel, and the two maidservants. I put the maidservants and their children in front, Leah and her children next, and Rachel and Joseph at the rear. I went ahead and bowed to the ground seven times as Esau approached. Esau; however, ran and embraced me; threw his arms around my neck, and kissed me. We both cried and then Esau noticed the rest of my family as they approached. He asked, "Who is this with you?" I answered, "These are the children God has graciously given your servant." The maidservants and their children greeted Esau; then Leah and her children; then Rachel and Joseph. Now I see that all my scheming was a total waste of time and it almost blew up in my face. Esau had already forgiven me and I didn't even know it. I also understand, it could have been offensive to him and looked as if I had not changed a bit. God fixed everything, just like He said He would. I just needed to trust Him. Esau said, "Let's make our way back home and I'll lead the way." The children are tired, the flocks need to rest, if I drive them any harder, they will die. You go ahead, and we'll take our time and meet you at Seir." I replied. Esau headed out and when they were out of sight, I took a detour and went on to Succoth. We settled there, and I built a house for my family and shelters for my livestock. Later, we went to Shechem. I purchased a plot of land from the sons of Hamor for a hundred pieces of silver. I pitched my tents and settled there. I set up an altar and called it El-Elohe-Israel (Mighty God of Israel).

As time passed, the voice of the Lord came to me and said, "Arise, go up to Bethel, and settle there, and build an altar there to Me." So, I told everyone, "Get rid of the foreign gods that you might have. Purify yourselves and change your garments. Then we will go to Bethel. I will build an altar there to the God who answered me in my day of distress. He has been with me wherever I have gone." After we arrived at Bethel, I built an altar as God instructed, and called that place El-Bethel, because it was there that God had revealed Himself to me as I fled from my brother. When I finished the altar, God appeared to me again and blessed me. He said, "I am God Almighty. Be fruitful and multiply. A nation, even a company of nations; shall come from you, and kings shall descend from you. The land that I gave to Abraham and Isaac I will give to you, and I will give this land to your descendants after you." Then He departed. I set up a pillar in the place where God had spoken to me, a stone marker, and I poured out a drink offering on it and anointed it with oil.

A little more than eight months later, we're on the move again. This move is a little different though. It might not be the best timing, because Rachel is pregnant. Not far from Ephrath, Rachel began to give birth, and her labor was very difficult. During her severe labor, the midwife said to her, "Do not be afraid, for you are having another son." After he was born, Rachel named his Ben-oni (son of my sorrow), and then she died. I changed the boy's name to Benjamin (Son of the right side); then I buried my beloved Rachel. Why didn't I wait until after Rachel gave birth; to leave Bethel? Would that have even made a difference? Could I have prevented this? I have to make it back to my homeland, so it's time to pack up and move on. We got just beyond the tower of Edar and pitch the tents. While there, Ruben slept with my concubine Bilhah. I'll deal with Ruben later, because if I do it right now, I'm may just do something that I might regret. Well, maybe not really regret right at this moment. After such an offensive betrayal of my trust, he would honestly get what he deserves.

Now, these are the sons by which God had promised to make a great nation.

From Leah: Reuben- behold a son
             Simeon- to hear, listen
             Levi- accompany, joined to
             Judah- praise
             Issachar- there is a reward, my hire
             Zebulun- honor
             Dinah- avenged, judged and vindicated

From Bilhah: Dan- judge
             Naphtali- my struggle, my strife

From Zilpah Gad- fortunate, luck
             Asher- happy one

From Rachel: Joseph- he increases
             Benjamin- son of the right side

We finally made it back to Hebron. My father, Isaac is 180 years old and died soon after. Esau and I buried him there, and Esau returned to Seir and I stayed in Hebron. It seems there are some lessons learned, that are hard to unlearn. There's a little favoritism going on in my house. Honestly, it's more than a little. Joseph is the favorite, and I got the sense that his ten older brothers don't like him much. I know it's not necessarily right, and you would think I would know better having gone through this myself. I was mother's favorite, and Esau was father's, and you see how that played out. Logically, I get it; however, sometimes, emotions overrule logic. This just so happens to be one of those times. I mean, Joseph is the firstborn of my beloved Rachel! Joseph turned 17 and I gave him a coat of many colors. One day he went into the fields to tend to the flocks with Dan; Naphtali; Gad, and Asher. Oh, did I mention Joseph was a talebearer? He came home and told me about the mischief his brothers had gotten into while in the fields. Needless to say, they didn't like that much. One day Joseph told me of a dream that he had. He said, "I had a dream, the sun, and moon, and eleven stars bowed down to me." I rebuked him saying, "What is this dream that you have had? Will your mother and brothers and I in reality come and bow down to the ground before you?" His brothers were jealous of him, but I kept in mind what he had said.

Knowing how his brother's felt about him, I should have limited the time Joseph spent in the fields with his brothers, but he enjoyed tending the flocks and being around his older brothers. One day, Joseph went to the fields, with his brothers, and he didn't return. His brothers brought me his torn and bloody coat and told me he was attacked and killed by a vicious animal. I tore my clothes and wept bitterly. I put on sackcloth and mourned Joseph for a while. In fact, it was so bad, that my other children tried to comfort me, and I wouldn't allow it. I told them I would go to my grave mourning him.

Many years have passed since Joseph has been gone, and

now to add to my misery, there is a famine throughout the land. Now rumor has it, there is grain in Egypt. I sent all my sons except Benjamin down to Egypt to purchase grain. When my sons returned, Simeon was not with them. They told me what happened while in Egypt saying, "The man who is the lord of the land spoke harshly to us and accused us of spying on the country, but we told him, 'We are honest men, not spies. We are twelve brothers, sons of one father. One is dead, and the youngest is now with our father in the land of Canaan.' Then the man who is the lord of the land said to us, 'This is how I will know whether you are honest: Leave one brother with me, take food to relieve the hunger of your households, and go, but bring your youngest brother back to me so I will know that you are not spies, but honest men. Then I will give your brother back to you, and you can trade in the land.'" As everyone began to empty their sacks, they noticed that all their money had been put back. We were all disheartened. I said to them, "You have deprived me of my sons. Joseph is gone and Simeon is being held captive. Now you want to take Benjamin. Why is this happening to me?" Then Reuben said, "You may kill my two sons if I fail to bring him back to you. Put him in my care, and I will return him." I replied, "Benjamin will not go down there with you, Joseph is dead, and he is all I have left from Rachel. If any harm comes to him on your journey; you will cause me to die in my sorrow." When all the grain was gone, I told my sons to go back to Egypt to buy more grain. Judah said, "The man sternly warned us, 'You will not see my face again unless your brother is with you.' If you will send Benjamin with us; we will go down and buy food for you. If you will not send him; we will not go.'" "Why did you bring this trouble upon me?" I asked. "Why did you tell the man you had another brother?" They replied, "The man questioned us in detail about ourselves and our family: 'Is your father still alive? Do you have another brother?' We answered him accordingly. How could we possibly know that he would say, 'Bring your brother here'?" Judah said, "Send the boy

15

with me and we will go at once; so that we may live and not die. I will guarantee his safety. You may hold me personally responsible! If I do not bring him back, then let me bear the guilt before you all my life. If we had not waited, we could have come and gone twice by now." I guess I don't have much choice. I told them to take double the money so that you may return the money that was put back into your sacks. I said to them, "May God Almighty grant you mercy before the man so that he will release your other brother along with Benjamin. As for me, if I am grieved, I am grieved." Then they departed along with Benjamin. Several days later all eleven sons returned and said, "Joseph is still alive, and he is ruler over all the land of Egypt!" I was shocked. I wasn't sure if I believed them. When they told me everything that Joseph had said, and when I saw the wagons that Joseph had sent to bring me back; I was relieved and excited to be able to see him.

So, we set out for Egypt, and when we came to Beersheba, I offered sacrifices to the God of my father Isaac. That night God spoke to me in a vision: "Jacob, Jacob!" He said. "Here I am," I replied. "I am God. The God of your father. Do not be afraid to go down to Egypt, for I will make you into a great nation there. I will go down with you to Egypt, and I will surely bring you back, and Joseph's own hands will close your eyes." After that, we left Beersheba and continued to Egypt. I sent Judah ahead to get direction to Goshen. When we arrived in Goshen, Joseph met us there. We embraced and I wept profusely with joy. Then I said to Joseph, "Finally I can die, now that I have seen your face and know that you are still alive!" Later Joseph brought me to the palace and presented me to Pharaoh, and I blessed Pharaoh. "How old are you?" Pharaoh asked. "My pilgrimage has lasted 130 years," I replied. "My years have been few and hard, and they have not matched the years of the lives of my fathers." Then I blessed Pharaoh and departed. So, we settled in Goshen and God blessed us there. We prospered and grew in number. As time passed, I spoke with Joseph and said, "If I have found favor in your sight, put your hand under my thigh and promise me that you will show me kindness and faithfulness. Do not bury me in Egypt, but carry me out of Egypt and bury me with my fathers." Joseph answered, "I will do as you have asked."

I lived another 17 years in Goshen, and now I'm 147 and on my death bed. Joseph came to see me one last time and when he entered my room, I mustered all my remaining strength to sit up in my bed. I told him, "God Almighty appeared to me at Bethel in the land of Canaan, and there He blessed me. He told me, 'Behold, I will make you fruitful and multiply you; I will make you a multitude of peoples, and will give this land to your descendants after you as an everlasting possession.' Now your two sons Ephraim and Manasseh shall be reckoned as mine, just as Reuben and Simeon are mine." I then told Joseph to bring me his sons so I could bless them. Joseph did as I asked and I kissed the boys and hugged them. I stretched out my right hand and put it on the head of Ephraim, the younger; and crossing my hands, put my left on Manasseh's head, although Manasseh was the firstborn. Then I blessed Joseph and said: "May the God before whom Abraham and Isaac walked, the God who has been my shepherd all my life to this day, the Angel who has redeemed me from all harm; may He bless these boys. May they be called by my name and the names of my fathers, and may they grow into a multitude upon the earth." When Joseph saw that I had placed his right hand on Ephraim's head, he was upset and took my hand to move it from Ephraim's head to Manasseh's. Joseph said, "Not so, my father!" "This one is the firstborn; put your right hand on his head." I refused. "I know, my son, I know!" I said. "He too shall become a people, and he too shall be great; nevertheless, his younger brother shall be greater than he, and his offspring shall become a multitude of nations." Then I said to Joseph, "I am about to die, but God will be with you and bring you back to the land of your fathers, and to you, as one who is above your brothers, I give the ridge of land that I took from the Amorites with my sword and bow."

It took a lot to arrive at this place. A lot of hard lessons learned, and a lot of issues to be rectified. God proved Himself faithful over and over, and as the time passed. He went from being the God of my fathers to my God. The more God changed my character, the stronger our relationship became. The end is near and I called all my sons together and prophesied unto them. Oh, nearly forgot: remember when I told you I'd handle Rueben's defilement of my bed later? Well, here it comes. "Come together and listen, O sons of Jacob; listen to your father Israel.

Reuben, you are my firstborn, my might, and the beginning of my strength, excelling in honor, excelling in power. Uncontrolled as the waters, you will no longer excel, because you went up to your father's bed, onto my couch and defiled it...

Simeon and Levi are brothers; their swords are weapons of violence. May I never enter their council; may I never join their assembly. For they kill men in their anger and exterminated oxen on a whim. Cursed be their anger, for it is strong, and their wrath, for it is cruel! I will disperse them in Jacob and scatter them in Israel...

Judah, your brothers shall praise you. Your hand shall be on the necks of your enemies; your father's sons shall bow down to you. Judah is a young lion, my son, you return from the prey. Like a lion, he crouches and lies down; like a lioness, who dares to rouse him? The scepter will not depart from Judah, nor the staff from between his feet, until Shiloh comes and the allegiance of the nations is his. He ties his donkey to the vine, his colt to the choicest branch. He washes his garments in wine, his robes in the blood of grapes. His eyes are darker than wine, and his teeth are whiter than milk...

Zebulun shall dwell by the seashore and become a harbor for ships; his border shall extend to Sidon...

Issachar is a strong donkey, lying down between the fireplaces. He saw that his resting place was good and that

his land was pleasant, so he bent his shoulder to the burden and submitted to labor as a servant...

Dan shall provide justice for his people as one of the tribes of Israel. He will be a serpent by the road, a viper in the path, that bites the horse's heels so that its rider tumbles backward. I await Your salvation, O LORD...

Gad will be attacked by raiders, but he will attack their rear...

Asher's food will be rich; he shall provide royal delicacies...

Naphtali is a doe set free that bears beautiful fawns...

Joseph is a fruitful vine, a fruitful vine by a spring, whose branches scale the wall. The archers attacked him with bitterness and aimed in hostility. Yet he steadied his bow, and his strong arms were tempered by the hands of the Mighty One of Jacob, in the name of the Shepherd, the Rock of Israel, by the God of your father who helps you, and by the Almighty who blesses you, with blessings of the heavens above, with blessings of the depths below, with blessings of the breasts and womb. The blessings of your father have surpassed the blessings of the ancient mountains and the bounty of the everlasting hills. May they rest on the head of Joseph, on the brow of the prince of his brothers...

Benjamin is a ravenous wolf; in the morning he devours the prey, in the evening he divides the plunder."

Now, one last thing before I die. Bury me with my fathers in the cave in the field of Ephron the Hittite. The cave is in the field of Machpelah near Mamre, in the land of Canaan. This is the field Abraham purchased from Ephron the Hittite as a burial site. There Abraham and his wife Sarah are buried, there Isaac and his wife Rebekah are buried, and there I buried Leah. With that, I breathed my last breath and died.

Moses: A Journey of Detours

In a perfect world, the shortest distance between two points is a straight line. However, as you're about to see, my life is anything but perfect. My life's journey was full of twists and turns, ups and downs, and the detours are many. In fact, one could even conclude that I was a reluctant participant, to begin with. I guess curiosity just got the best of me. One thing you can certainly count on: this ride is anything but dull! In fact, I would say it's better than one of those contraptions, you call a rollercoaster. So, fasten your seatbelt and enjoy the ride.

It all began, one day when I went from the comfort of my mother's arms to floating down a river in a basket. I would end up at Pharaoh's palace, in the arms of his daughter. Now what I didn't know, but would later find out is that Pharaoh had ordered all male Israelite babies killed, that my mother hid me from the soldiers carrying out those orders, and when she could no longer hide me, she placed me in the basket, and my sister watched me float down the Nile river to the bank outside the palace. So, the very thing used to destroy so many innocent lives would also be the same thing to save one very important life: mine. Not only did GOD spare my life, but he also worked it out that I would be nursed by my mother. Oh yeah! I almost forgot, my mother, got paid to nurse me.

Pharaoh's daughter named me Moses meaning, "I drew him out of the water." Needless to say, as I grew, I received the best education of the day and enjoyed all the luxuries of a royal. As I grew to be a young man, I walked out among the Hebrews and observed their hard labor. I later saw an Egyptian, mercilessly beating one of the slaves. I looked around and saw no one, so I hit the Egyptian, killing him. I didn't think I had hit him that hard, but I obviously had. I buried his body in the sand and went back to the palace as if nothing had happened. The next day I went out and saw two Hebrews fighting. I asked the one in the wrong, "Why are you attacking your fellow Hebrew?" The man replied, "Who made you ruler and judge over us? Are you planning to kill me as you killed the Egyptian?" I got scared and thought, my secret would get out. As you could probably guess it wasn't long before Pharaoh found out that I had killed an Egyptian and wanted me dead.

I fled Egypt, and came to a well in Midian and sat down to rest. Now the priest of Midian had seven daughters, and they came to draw water and fill the troughs to water their father's flock. Some shepherds came along and started to chase them away. I stood up and came to their rescue and watered their flock. The young ladies returned home to their father and told him what happened. He sent them back to invite me to his home. I stayed with him for a while and eventually married his daughter Zipporah. According to the time of life Zipporah gave birth to a son whom we named Gershom, for I said, "I have become a stranger in a strange land."

As time passed, the king of Egypt died. The Israelites groaned and cried out under the burden of slavery, and their cry for deliverance ascended to God. God heard their groaning and remembered His covenant with Abraham, Isaac, and Jacob. Meanwhile, I was watching the flock of Jethro, the priest of Midian. I led them to the far side of the wilderness and came to Horeb, the mountain of God. There the angel of the LORD appeared to me in a burning bush. I saw the bush on fire, but it was not consumed. Needless to say, my curiosity got the best of me and I had to see how this bush was on fire and not consumed. Someone called out to me from within the bush, "Moses, Moses!" Now I'm thinking to myself, what kind of craziness is this? The better part of wisdom says I should be going back down the mountain! Who, or what is talking to me, out of this bush (that's on FIRE)? I must be losing my mind. He continued saying, "Do not come any closer, take off your sandals, because the place where you are standing is holy ground. I am the God of your father, the God of Abraham, Isaac, and Jacob." I hid my face because I was afraid to look at God. He said, "Go back to Egypt, for all the men who sought to kill you are dead. I have seen the misery of My people in Egypt. I have heard them crying out because of their oppressors, and I am aware of their sufferings. I have come down to rescue them from the hand of the Egyptians. I will bring them up out of that land to a good land, a land flowing with milk and honey. Therefore, go! I am sending you to Pharaoh to bring My people, out of Egypt."

I said, "Whoa! Wait a minute! I knew I should have walked away when I had the chance. Who am I, that I should go to Pharaoh and bring the Israelites out of Egypt?" God replied, "I will surely be with you, and this will be the sign to you that I have sent you. When you have brought the people out of Egypt, all of you will worship Me on this mountain." Then I asked, "Suppose I go to the Israelites and tell them, 'The God of your fathers has sent me to you.' and they ask me, 'What is His name?' What should I tell them?'" God replied, "I AM WHO I AM. That is what you are to tell them: 'I AM has sent me, the God of Abraham, Isaac, and Jacob.'" Assemble the elders of Israel and say to them, 'The LORD, the God of your fathers has appeared to me and said: 'I have surely attended to you and have seen what has been done to you in Egypt. I have promised to bring you up out of your affliction in Egypt, and into the land of the Canaanites, Hittites, Amorites, Perizzites, Hivites, and Jebusites.' They will listen to what you say. You must go with them to the king of Egypt and tell him, 'The LORD, the God of the Hebrews, has met with us. Now let us take a three-day journey into the wilderness, so that we may sacrifice to the LORD our God.' I know that the king of Egypt will not allow you to go unless a mighty hand makes him. So, I will stretch out My hand and strike the

Egyptians with all the wonders I will perform among them. After that, he will release you. I will give these people such favor in the sight of the Egyptians that when you leave, you will not go away empty-handed."

"What if they refuse to believe me or listen to my voice? They may say, 'The LORD has not appeared to you.'" God replied, "What is that in your hand?" "A staff," I replied. "Throw it on the ground," said the Lord. I did so, and it became a snake, and I ran from it. Stretch out your hand and grab it by the tail," the LORD said. I did so reluctantly and caught the snake, and it turned back into a staff. "This is so that they may believe that the LORD, the God of their fathers has appeared to you. Furthermore, put your hand inside your cloak." I put my hand inside my cloak, and when I took it out, it was leprous, white as snow. "Put your hand back inside your cloak," said the LORD, and I did so, and when I took it out, it was restored, like the rest of my skin. Then the LORD said, "If they refuse to believe you or heed the witness of the first sign, they may believe that of the second. If they do not believe these two signs or listen to your voice, take some water from the Nile and pour it on the dry ground, and it will become blood on the ground."

Now I'm thinking to myself if only I hadn't looked at that bush!! This is very overwhelming. Let me try one more excuse to get out of this. I said, "Please, Lord, I have never been eloquent. Neither in the past nor since You have spoken to me. Surely you can hear, I stutter a lot." The LORD said forcefully, "Who gave man his mouth? Or who makes him mute or deaf, sighted or blind? Am I not, the LORD? Now go! I will help you as you speak, and I will teach you what to say." "Please, Lord, send someone else." I pleaded, and that was the straw that broke the camel's back. God got angry with me, and He said, "Is Aaron the Levite your brother? I know that he can speak well, and he is now on his way to meet you. He will be very happy to see you. Tell him to speak the words that I told you. I will help both of you to speak, and I will teach you what to do. He will speak to the people for you. He will be your spokesman, and it will be as if you were God to him. Take this staff in your hand so that you can perform signs with it."

After that, I went back to Jethro and said to him, "Please let me return to my brothers in Egypt and see if they are still alive." Jethro replied, "Go in peace." So, I took my wife and sons, put them on a donkey, and headed back to Egypt. On our journey, we stopped at an inn. The LORD confronted me and was about to kill me because my son, Eliezer had not been circumcised according to Hebrew customs. In her frustration with that custom, Zipporah, pulled out a knife and cut off the boy's foreskin. God spared my life, but my wife took the boys back to Midian in a rage. The LORD instructed me, "When you go back to Egypt, see that you perform before Pharaoh all the wonders that I have put within your power. However, I will harden his heart so that he will not let the people go. Then tell Pharaoh, "This is what the LORD says: 'Israel is My firstborn son, and I told you to let My son go so that he may worship Me. You have refused to let him go, so I will kill your firstborn son!'"

After a while, Aaron met me at the mountain of God and kissed me. I told him everything the LORD said, and all the signs He had commanded me to perform. Once arriving in Goshen, Aaron and I went and assembled all the elders of the Israelites. Aaron relayed everything that the LORD had said to me. I performed the signs before the people, and they believed. When they heard that the LORD had paid attention to the Israelites and had seen their affliction, they bowed down and worshiped. After that, Aaron and I went to Pharaoh and said, "This is what the LORD, the God of Israel, says: 'Let My people go, so that they may hold a feast to Me in the wilderness.'" Pharaoh replied, "Who is the LORD that I should obey His voice and let Israel go? I do not know the LORD, and I will not let Israel go." That same day Pharaoh commanded the taskmasters of the people and their foremen: "You shall no longer supply the people with straw for making bricks. They must gather their own, and you will require the same quota of bricks as before; do not reduce it. For they are lazy, that is why they are crying out, 'Let us go and sacrifice to our God.' Make the work harder on the men so they will be occupied and pay no attention to these lies." Then the Israelite foremen, whom Pharaoh's taskmasters had set over the people, were beaten and asked, "Why have you not fulfilled your quota of bricks yesterday or today, as you did before?" The foremen then confronted me and Aaron. "May the LORD look upon you and judge you," the foremen said, "for you have made us a stench before Pharaoh and his officials. You have placed in their hand a sword to kill us!" I called out to the LORD, "LORD, why have You brought trouble upon this people? Is this why You sent me? Ever since I went to Pharaoh to speak in Your name, he has brought trouble on this people, and You have not delivered them." God replied, "Now you will see what I will do to Pharaoh. Because of My mighty hand, he will let them go. I am the LORD. I appeared to Abraham, to Isaac, and Jacob as God Almighty, but I did not reveal Myself to them by My name, 'JEHOVAH.' I also established My covenant with them to give them the land of Canaan. The land where they had lived as foreigners. Furthermore, I have heard the groaning of the Israelites, whom the Egyptians are enslaving, and I have remembered My covenant. Tell them: 'I am the LORD, and I will bring you out from under the yoke of the Egyptians and deliver you from your bondage. I will redeem you with an outstretched arm and with mighty acts of judgment. I will take you as My people, and I will be your God. Then you will know that I am the LORD your God.'" So, I delivered this message to the Israelites, but because of their spirits were broken, they did not listen to me. Then God commanded, "Go and tell Pharaoh to let the Israelites go out of his land. Speak all that I command

you, and Aaron must declare it to Pharaoh so that he will
let the Israelites go out of his land. I will harden Pharaoh's
heart, and I will multiply My signs and wonders in the
land of Egypt. I will lay My hand on Egypt, and by mighty
acts of judgment I will bring My people out of Egypt." We
did as God commanded and Pharaoh requested to see a
miracle. Aaron threw my staff down before Pharaoh and
his officials, and it became a serpent. Pharaoh then called
the wise men and sorcerers and magicians of Egypt, and
they also did the same things by their magic. Each one
threw down his staff, and it became a serpent. but Aaron's
serpent swallowed up the others, and as Aaron reached
out to grab the serpent by its tail it turned back into a staff.
Pharaoh's heart was still hardened, and he did not listen
to us. Then the LORD said to me, "Go to Pharaoh in the
morning. As you see him walking out to the water; wait
on the bank of the Nile to meet him. Take the staff that is
in your hand, and say to him, 'The LORD, the God of the
Hebrews, has sent me to tell you: Let My people go, so that
they may worship Me in the wilderness.'"

I met Pharaoh at the river, and said to him, "This is what
the LORD said: 'By this, you will know that I am the
LORD.' Behold, with the staff in my hand I will strike the
water of the Nile, and it will turn to blood. The fish in the
Nile will die. The river will stink, and the Egyptians will
be unable to drink its water." Then Aaron took my staff
and stretched his hand over the waters of Egypt; over their
rivers; canals; ponds and reservoirs, and they become
blood. Even the water in the vessels of wood and stone
became blood. Then the magicians of Egypt did the same
things by their magic. Pharaoh's heart was again hardened,
and he would not listen to us.

Seven days later, the LORD said to me, "Go to Pharaoh and
tell him, Let My people go, so that they may worship Me. If
you refuse to do so, I will plague your entire country with
frogs." Of course, Pharaoh refused, so Aaron stretched out

his hand with my staff over the rivers, canals, and ponds, and frogs began to come up onto the land, and into the palace. They were in his bedroom and on his bed. They were in the houses of his officials and all the people. Again, Pharaoh summoned his magicians and they did the same. When the frogs became unnerving Pharaoh sent for us and said, "Pray to the LORD to take the frogs away from me and my people. Then I will let your people go, that they may sacrifice to the LORD." I said to Pharaoh, "You can decide when I pray that the frogs will be taken away from you and your houses." "Tomorrow," Pharaoh answered. "It will be as you say, the frogs will depart from you and your houses and your officials and your people. They will remain in the Nile alone, so that you may know that there is no one like the LORD our God." After we left Pharaoh, I called out to the LORD for help, and the LORD did as I requested, and the frogs in the houses, the courtyards, and the fields died. The people piled them into countless piles, and there was a terrible smell in the land. When Pharaoh saw the frogs were gone, he hardened his heart and didn't keep his word.

Then the LORD said to me, "Tell Aaron, 'Stretch out your staff and strike the dust of the earth. It will turn into swarms of gnats throughout the land of Egypt.'" Aaron did so, and the dust of the earth turned into gnats throughout the land. The magicians tried to produce gnats using their magic, but they couldn't. The magicians said, "This is the finger of God", but Pharaoh would not listen to them.

Then the LORD said to me, "Get up early in the morning, and when Pharaoh goes out to the water, stand before him and tell him, this is what the LORD said: 'Let My people go, so that they may worship Me. If not, I will send swarms of flies upon you. I will give special treatment to the land of Goshen. where My people live; no flies will be found there. In this, you will know that I, the LORD, am in the land." The next day, thick swarms of flies poured

28

into Pharaoh's palace and the houses of his officials. Then Pharaoh summoned me and Aaron and said, "Go, sacrifice to your God within this land." I replied, "It would not be right to do that. We must take a three-day journey into the wilderness and sacrifice to the LORD our God as He commands us." Pharaoh answered, "I will let you go and sacrifice to the LORD your God in the wilderness, but you must not go very far. Now, pray for me." "As soon as I leave you, I will pray to the LORD, so that tomorrow the swarms of flies will depart from you; however, you better not act deceitfully, and refuse to let us go and sacrifice to the LORD." I left Pharaoh and prayed to the LORD, and the LORD did as I requested. He removed the swarms of flies; not one fly remained. Yet Pharaoh hardened his heart again, and he would not let us go.

Then the LORD said to me "Go to Pharaoh and tell him this is what the LORD says: 'Let My people go, so that they may worship Me. If you refuse to let them go and continue to restrain them, the hand of the LORD will bring a severe plague on your livestock in the field; on your horses; donkeys; camels; herds and flocks, but He will make a distinction between the livestock of Israel and the livestock of Egypt. No animal belonging to the Israelites will die.'" The next day the LORD did just that. All the livestock of the Egyptians died, but not one animal belonging to the Israelites died. So, Pharaoh sent officials, who saw that none of the livestock of the Israelites had died, but Pharaoh's heart was hardened, and he would not let the people go.

Then the LORD said to me and Aaron, "Take handfuls of soot from the furnace; in the sight of Pharaoh, and toss it into the air. It will become fine dust over all the land of Egypt; festering boils will break out on man and beast throughout the land." We did as the Lord commanded and festering boils broke out on both man and beast. The magicians could not stand before me, because the boils had broken out on them and all the Egyptians. Then the LORD said to me, "Get up early in the morning, stand before Pharaoh, and tell him, this is what the LORD, the God of the Hebrews, said: 'Let My people go, so that they may worship Me. Otherwise, I will send all My plagues against you and your people, so you may know that there is no one like Me in all the earth.'

At this time tomorrow, I will rain down the worst hail that has ever fallen on Egypt. So, give orders now to shelter your livestock and everything you have in the field. Every man or beast that remains in the field and is not brought inside will die.'" Those officials who feared the word of the LORD hurried to bring their servants and livestock to shelter, but those who disregarded the word of the LORD left their servants and livestock in the field. Then the LORD said to me, "Stretch out your hand toward heaven, so that hail may fall on all the land of Egypt: on man and beast and every plant of the field throughout the land." I stretched out my staff toward heaven, and the LORD sent thunder and hail, and lightning struck the earth. The hail fell and the lightning continued flashing through it. The hail was so severe that nothing like it had ever been seen in all the land of Egypt. The hail struck down everything in the field, both man and beast. It beat down every plant of the field and stripped every tree, but the hail did not fall in the land of Goshen. Then Pharaoh called for me and Aaron. He said, "This time I have sinned. The LORD is righteous, and I and my people are wicked. Pray to the LORD, for there has been enough of God's thunder and hail. I will let you go. You don't need to stay any longer." I said to him, "When I leave the city, I will spread out my hands to the LORD. The thunder will cease, and there will be no more hail, so that you may know that the Earth is the LORD's, but I know that you still do not fear the LORD our God." When Pharaoh saw that the hail and thunder had stopped, he sinned again and hardened his heart.

Then the LORD said to me, "Go to Pharaoh, for I have hardened his heart and the hearts of his officials, that I may perform these miraculous signs of Mine among them. Also, you may tell your children and grandchildren how severely I dealt with the Egyptians, and that all of you may know that I am the LORD." So, Aaron and I went to Pharaoh and said, "This is what the LORD, the God of the Hebrews, says: 'How long will you refuse to humble yourself before Me? Let My people go, so that they may worship Me. If you refuse to let them go, I will bring locusts into your territory tomorrow. They will cover the face of the land so that no one can see it. They will devour whatever is left after the hail and eat every tree that grows in your fields. They will fill your houses and the houses of all your officials and every Egyptian. It will be something neither your fathers nor your grandfathers have seen since the day they came into this land.'" Then we left Pharaoh's presence. After a few minutes, we were brought back to Pharaoh. "Go, worship the LORD your God," he said. "But who exactly will be going?" "We will go with our young and old," I replied. "We will go with our sons and daughters, and with our flocks and herds, for we must hold a feast to the LORD." Then Pharaoh told us, "May the LORD be with you if I ever let you go with your little ones. Undoubtedly, you are up to no good. Only the men may go and worship the LORD since that is what you have been requesting", and we were sent from Pharaoh's presence. Then the LORD said to me, "Stretch out your hand over the land of Egypt, that the locusts may swarm over it and devour every plant in the land: everything that the hail did not destroy." I stretched out my staff over Egypt, and throughout that day and night, the LORD sent an east wind across the land. By morning the land was full of locusts. They covered the face of all the land until it was black. They consumed all the plants on the ground and all the fruit on the trees that the hail had left behind. Nothing green was left on any tree or plant in all the land. Pharaoh quickly summoned us and said, "I have sinned against the LORD your God and you.

Please forgive my sin once more and appeal to the LORD your God, so that He will remove this destruction from me." So, we left the palace and appealed to the LORD. He changed the wind to a very strong west wind that carried off the locusts and blew them into the Red Sea. However, the LORD hardened Pharaoh's heart yet again, and he would not let the Israelites go.

Then the LORD said to me, "Stretch out your hand toward heaven so that darkness will spread over the land of Egypt: a tangible darkness." I did as I was commanded and darkness fell on Egypt for three days. No one could see each other, and for three days no one left his place. Yet all the Israelites had light in their dwellings. Then Pharaoh summoned me and said, "Go, worship the LORD. Even your little ones may go with you, but your flocks and herds must stay behind." Then I replied, "You must also provide us with sacrifices and burnt offerings to present to the LORD our God. Even our livestock must go with us; not a hoof will be left behind, for we will need some of them to worship the LORD our God, and we will not know how we are to worship the LORD until we arrive." Then the LORD hardened Pharaoh's heart yet again, and he was not willing to let them go. "Leave me!" Pharaoh said. "Make sure I never see your face again, for on the day I see your face, you will die." "As you wish; I will never see your face again", I replied.

Then the LORD said to me, "I will bring upon Pharaoh and Egypt one more plague. After that, he will allow you to leave this place. When he lets you go, he will drive you out completely. Now announce to the people that men and women alike should ask their neighbors for articles of silver and gold." The LORD gave the people favor in the sight of the Egyptians. Moreover, I was highly regarded in Egypt by Pharaoh's officials and by the people. So, I declared, "This is what the LORD said 'About midnight I will go throughout Egypt, and every firstborn son in the land of Egypt will die; from the firstborn of Pharaoh; to the firstborn of the servant girl behind the hand mill; as well as the firstborn of all the cattle. Then a great cry will go out over all the land of Egypt, such as never has been heard before, and will never be heard again. Nevertheless, among all the Israelites, not even a dog will snarl at man or beast.' Then you will know that the LORD makes a distinction between Egypt and Israel.

Later that day, the LORD said to me and Aaron, "This month is the beginning of months for you; it shall be the first month of the year. Tell the whole congregation of Israel that on the tenth day of this month, each man must select a lamb for his family, one per household. If the household is too small for a whole lamb, they are to share with the nearest neighbor, based on the number of people, and apportion the lamb accordingly. Your lamb must be an unblemished-year-old male, and you may take it from the sheep or the goats. You must care for it until the fourteenth day of the month when the whole assembly of the congregation of Israel will slaughter the animals at twilight. They are to take some of the blood and put it on the two side posts and tops of the doorframes of the houses in which they eat the lambs. They are to eat the meat that night, roasted over the fire, along with unleavened bread and bitter herbs. Do not eat any of the meat raw or cooked in boiling water. Do not leave any of it until morning; you must burn up any part that is left over. This is how you are to eat it: you must be fully dressed for travel, with your sandals on your feet and your staff in your hand. You are to eat in haste; it is the LORD's Passover. On that night I will pass through the land and strike down every firstborn male, both man and beast, and I will execute judgment against all the gods of Egypt. I am the LORD. The blood on the houses where you are staying will distinguish them; when I see the blood, I will pass over you. No plague will fall on you to destroy you when I strike the land of Egypt. This day will be a memorial for you, and you are to celebrate it as a feast to the LORD, and as a lasting ordinance for the generations to come. When your children ask you, 'What does this service mean to you?' you are to reply, 'It is the Passover sacrifice to the LORD, who passed over the houses of the Israelites in Egypt when He struck down the Egyptians and spared our homes.'" Then the people bowed down and worshiped, and then went to do what the LORD had commanded.

At midnight the LORD struck down every firstborn male in the land of Egypt, from the firstborn of Pharaoh to the firstborn of the prisoner in the dungeon, as well as all the firstborn among the livestock. During the night Pharaoh got up, he and all his officials and all the Egyptians—and there was loud wailing in Egypt; for there was no house without someone dead. Then Pharaoh summoned me and Aaron by night and said, "Get up, leave my people, both you and the Israelites! Go, worship the LORD as you have requested. Take your flocks and herds as well, just as you have said, and depart!" In order to get them out of the land quickly, the Egyptians urged the people on. "For otherwise," they said, "we are all going to die!" So, the people took their unleavened dough, carrying it on their shoulders in kneading bowls wrapped in clothing.

The duration of the Israelites' stay in Egypt was 430 years, and all the LORD's divisions went out of the land of Egypt. After 400 years of captivity in Egypt, the consensus was, it felt good to be free. We journeyed from Rameses to Succoth with about 600,000 men on foot, besides women and children. A mixed multitude of Egyptians that feared God and slaves of other nationalities also went up with us. As a side note, be careful who you keep company with. You will soon see that evil communication corrupts good manners. There was also a great drove of livestock, both flocks, and herds. I took the bones of Joseph with me because Joseph made the sons of Israel swear a solemn oath when he said, "God will surely attend to you, and then you must carry my bones with you from this place."

God led us by the way of the wilderness toward the Red Sea, and we left the land of Egypt with the armed men in front. Now the ten plagues that the Lord brought down upon Egypt were something to behold, but they paled in comparison to the way He led us on our journey. He went before us in a pillar of cloud by day, and in a pillar of fire to give us light at night, so that we could travel by day or night. Sure, we've all looked up into the sky and seen clouds, but this was a pillar/ column, stretching from the ground, upward, and it moved before us. Even more impressive than that, a column of fire! Impressive, astonishing, amazing, words just can't describe such a sight. We set out from Succoth and camped at Etham on the edge of the wilderness. Then the Lord said to me, "Tell the people to turn back and encamp before Pi-hahiroth, between Migdol and the sea. You are to encamp by the sea, directly opposite Baal-zephon. Pharaoh will say of the Israelites, 'They are wandering the land aimlessly; the wilderness has boxed them in', and I will harden Pharaoh's heart so that he will pursue you. However, I will be honored by men through Pharaoh and all his army, and the Egyptians will know that I am the LORD." We did as the Lord had spoken to me.

As we camped by the sea near Pi-hahiroth, all Pharaoh's horses and chariots, horsemen and troops approached from behind, and the people were terrified and cried out to the Lord. They began to murmur and said, "Was it because there were no graves in Egypt that you brought us into the wilderness to die? What have you done to us by bringing us out of Egypt? Did we not say to you in Egypt, 'Leave us alone so that we may serve the Egyptians'? For it would have been better for us to serve the Egyptians than to die in the wilderness." All I could do is shake my head. See how quickly they have forgotten the severity of their captivity. After all, the Lord has done to end our captivity; after saying Pharaoh would come after us, they still don't believe God. I told them, "Do not be afraid. Stand still and you will see the salvation of the LORD, which He will provide for you today. The Egyptians you see today, you will never see again. The LORD will fight for you; you need only to be still." Then the LORD said to me, "Why are you crying out to Me? Tell the congregation to go forward. As for you, lift your staff and stretch out your hand over the sea and divide it, so that you can go through the sea on dry ground. I will harden the hearts of the Egyptians one last time so that they will come in after you."

Then the Angel of God, who had gone before us, withdrew and went behind us. The pillar of cloud also moved from before us and stood behind us, so that it came between the camps of Egypt and Israel. The cloud was as a blanket of darkness to them, but it lit up the night for us. I stretched out my hand over the sea, and all that night a strong east wind divided the waters, and we went through the sea on dry ground. At daybreak, as we crossed the sea, the pillar lifted, and the Egyptians chased after us. All Pharaoh's horses, chariots, and horsemen, and soldiers followed us into the sea. Then the LORD looked down on the army of the Egyptians from the pillar of fire and cloud, and He threw their camp into disarray. He caused their chariot wheels to wobble so that they had difficulty driving. "Let us flee from the Israelites," said the Egyptians, "for the LORD is fighting for them against us!" The LORD spoke to me, "Stretch out your hand over the sea, so that the waters may flow back over the Egyptians and their chariots and horsemen." I stretched out my hand over the sea, and the sea returned to its normal state. While the Egyptians were retreating, the LORD swept them into the sea. The waters flowed back and covered the entire army of Pharaoh that had chased us into the sea. Not one of them survived. When we saw the great power, the LORD had shown over the Egyptians, the people feared the LORD and believed in Him and me.

From the Red Sea, we went out into the Desert of Shur. For three days we walked in the desert without finding water. When we came to Marah, we could not drink the water there because it was bitter. So, the people grumbled, saying, "What are we going to drink? I cried out to the LORD. He showed me a log, and when I cast it into the water, it was sweetened. There the LORD made for us a statute and an ordinance saying, "If you will listen carefully to the voice of the LORD your God, and do what is right in My eyes, and pay attention to My commands, and keep all My statutes, I will not bring on you any of the diseases I inflicted on the Egyptians. For I am the LORD who heals you." Then we went to Elim, where there were twelve springs of water and seventy palm trees, and we camped there by the waters. On the fifteenth day of the second month after we had left the land of Egypt, we set out from Elim and came to the Desert of Sin, which is between Elim and Sinai. Pay close attention here, or you'll miss a valuable lesson about the company you keep! There in the desert, they all grumbled against me and Aaron saying, "If only we had died by the LORD's hand in the land of Egypt!" they said. "There we sat by pots of meat and ate our fill of bread, but you have brought us into this desert to starve this whole assembly to death!" Now think back to the bitterness of slavery. Where was there ever a mention of pots of meat, or having our fill of bread? For 430 years the burden of slavery grew increasingly worse. Eventually, it got to be so horrific that they wanted to kill me for confronting Pharaoh on their behalf. They didn't cry out, "Moses, leave us alone, because the meat and the bread are so good, we don't mind the slavery." They cried out, "You have made us a stench to the Egyptians, and they want to kill us with swords." They have taken the memories of the mixed multitude and made them, their own.

Then the LORD said to me, "Behold, I will rain down bread from heaven for you. Each day the people are to go out and gather enough for that day. This way I will test whether

37

or not they will follow My instructions. On the sixth day, when they prepare what they bring in, it will be twice as much as they gather before." So, Aaron and I said to all the people, "This evening you will know that it was the LORD who brought you out of the land of Egypt, and in the morning, you will see the LORD's glory, because He has heard your grumbling against Him. For who are we that you should grumble against us? Your grumblings are not against us but the LORD." Then I said to the whole congregation, "Come before the LORD, for He has heard your grumbling.'" When the people heard these things, they looked toward the desert, and there in a cloud the glory of the LORD appeared. Then the LORD said to me, "I have heard the grumbling of the Israelites. Tell them, 'In the morning you will be filled with bread. Then you will know that I am the LORD your God.'" In the morning there was a layer of dew around the camp. When the layer of dew had evaporated, there were thin flakes on the desert floor, as fine as frost on the ground. When the Israelites saw it, they asked one another, "What is it?", because they did not know what it was. So, I told them, "It is the bread that the LORD has given you to eat, and no one may keep any of it until morning." Of course, they did not listen to me; some people left part of it until morning, and it became full of maggots and began to smell. To say I was angry with them would be an understatement. On the seventh day some of the people went out to gather bread, even though I had previously instructed them not to, but they did anyway and did not find anything.

We moved from place to place as the Lord led us, and we camped at Rephidim, but there was no water for the people to drink. So, the people complained to me saying, "Give us water to drink." "Why do you complain to me?" I replied. "Why do you test the LORD?" The people were thirsty, and they continued to grumble: "Why have you brought us out of Egypt—to kill us and our children and livestock with thirst?" Then I cried out to the LORD, "What should I do

with these people? A little more and they will stone me!"
Now I know I shouldn't have cried out to God like that,
but these people were starting to get on my nerves with
their constant complaining. They complained about bitter
water, and the Lord cleaned it up so they could drink.
They cried about being hungry, God gave them manna in
the morning. Can't they see, that God will provide for us
while we journey to the promised land? Now here they
are complaining again. If you remember, I didn't want
this job anyway. God is going to have to do something.
The LORD spoke to me, "Walk on ahead of the people and
take some of the elders of Israel with you. Take along in
your hand the staff with which you struck the Nile, and go.
Behold, I will stand there before you by the rock at Horeb;
when you strike the rock, water will come out of it for the
people to drink." So, I did this in the sight of the elders of
Israel. I named the place Massah and Meribah because the
Israelites quarreled, and because they tested the LORD,
saying, "Is the LORD among us or not?"

After this, the Amalekites came and attacked us at
Rephidim. So, I said to Joshua, "Choose some of our men
and go out to fight the Amalekites. Tomorrow I will stand
on the hilltop with the staff of God in my hand." Joshua
did as instructed, and fought against the Amalekites, while
Aaron, Hur, and I went up to the top of the hill. As long as
I held up my hands, Israel prevailed; but when I lowered
them, Amalek prevailed. So, Aaron and Hur raised my
hands and held them until sunset, and Joshua defeated
the Amalekites. Then the LORD said to me "Write this
on a scroll as a reminder and recite it to Joshua because
I will utterly remove the memory of Amalek from under
heaven." Then I built an altar and called the name of it
Jehovahnissi: meaning the Lord is my banner.

Now Jethro, the priest of Midian, heard about all that
God had done, and how the LORD had brought Israel out
of Egypt. He, along with Zipporah and my sons, came to

me in the desert, where we encamped at the mountain of God. The next day I took my seat to judge the people, and they stood around me from morning until evening. When Jethro saw this, he asked, "What is this that you are doing to the people? Why do you sit alone as the judge, with all the people standing around you from morning till evening?" I replied, "Because the people come to me to inquire of God, and whenever they have a dispute, it is brought to me to judge, and I make known to them the statutes and laws of God." Then Jethro said, "What you are doing is not good. Surely you and these people will wear yourselves out. This task is too cumbersome for you. You cannot handle it alone. So, listen to me; I will give you some advice, and may God be with you. You must be the people's representative before God and bring their concerns to Him. Teach them the statutes and laws. Show them the way to live and the work they must do. Furthermore, select capable men from among the people: God-fearing, trustworthy men who hate dishonest gain. Appoint them over the people as leaders of thousands, of hundreds, of fifties, and tens. Let these men judge the people at all times. Then they can bring you any major issue, but all minor cases they can judge on their own. If you follow this advice and God so directs you, you will be able to endure, and all the people can go home in peace." I listened to Jethro and did everything he said.

In the third month, on the same day of the month that we had left Egypt, we came to the Desert of Sinai and camped in front of the mountain. Then I went up to God, and the LORD called to me from the mountain, "This is what you are to tell the house of Jacob and explain to the sons of Israel: 'You have seen with your own eyes what I did to Egypt, and how I carried you on eagles' wings and brought you to Myself. Now if you will obey My voice and keep My covenant, you will be My treasured possession out of all the nations. The whole earth is Mine, and you shall be a kingdom of priests and a holy nation unto Me.' These are the words that you are to speak to the Israelites." So, I went back and summoned the elders of the people and told them all that the LORD had commanded me, and all the people answered together, "We will do everything that the LORD has spoken." Then the LORD said to me, "Behold, I will come to you in a dense cloud, so that the people will hear when I speak with you, and they will always put their trust in you." I relayed the words of the people to the LORD. Then the LORD said, "Go to the people and consecrate them today and tomorrow. They must wash their clothes, and be prepared by the third day, for on the third day I will come down on Mount Sinai in the sight of all the people. You are to set up a boundary for the people around the mountain and tell them, 'Be careful not to go up on the mountain or touch its base. Whoever touches the mountain shall surely be put to death. No hand shall touch him, but he shall surely be stoned or shot with arrows; whether man or beast, he must not live.' Only when the ram's horn sounds a long blast may they go up the mountain."

Then the Lord called me to the top of the mountain, and He spoke all these words: "I am the LORD your God, who brought you out of the land of Egypt, and out of the house of slavery.

You shall have no other gods before Me.

You shall not make for yourself an idol of any kind, or an image of anything in the heavens above, on the earth beneath, or in the waters below. You shall not bow down to them or worship them. The LORD your God, is a jealous God, visiting the iniquity of the fathers on their children to the third and fourth generations of those who hate Me, but showing loving devotion to a thousand generations of those who love Me and keep My commandments.

You shall not take the name of the LORD your God in vain, for the LORD will not leave anyone unpunished who takes His name in vain.

Remember the Sabbath day and keep it holy. Six days you shall labor and do all your work, but the seventh day is a Sabbath to the LORD your God, on which you must not do any work: neither you; nor your son or daughter; nor your manservant or maidservant or livestock; nor the foreigner within your gates, because in six days the LORD made the heavens and the earth and the sea and all that is in them, but on the seventh day He rested. Therefore, the LORD blessed the Sabbath day and made it holy.

Honor your father and mother, so that your days may be long in the land the LORD your God is giving you.

You shall not murder.

You shall not commit adultery.

You shall not steal.

You shall not bear false witness against your neighbor.

You shall not covet your neighbor's house. You shall not covet your neighbor's wife, or his manservant or maidservant, nor his ox or donkey, or anything that belongs to your neighbor.

Then He continued saying "Treat your neighbor the way you want to be treated. If a serious injury results, then you must require a life for a life; an eye for an eye, a tooth for a tooth. Anyone that hits, or even disrespects their parent must surely die. You must not allow a sorceress to live. Whoever has sexual relations with an animal must surely be put to death. Whoever sacrifices to any god except the LORD alone must be utterly destroyed. You must not exploit or oppress a foreign resident, for you yourselves were foreigners in the land of Egypt. You must not mistreat any widow or orphan. If you do mistreat them, and they cry out to Me in distress, I will surely hear their cry. My anger will be kindled, and I will kill you with the sword; then your wives will be widows and your children will be orphans. You must not blaspheme God or curse the ruler of your people. You are to be My holy people. You must not eat the meat of a mauled animal found in the field; you are to throw it to the dogs. You shall not follow a crowd in wrongdoing. When you testify in a lawsuit, do not pervert justice by siding with a crowd. Stay far away from a false accusation. Do not kill the innocent or the just, for I will not acquit the guilty. Do not accept a bribe, for a bribe blinds those who see and twists the words of the righteous.

When I returned from the mountain, the people said, "We have witnessed the thunder and lightning, the sound of the trumpet, and the mountain in smoke, and were afraid and trembled and moved away from the mountain." They continued saying, "Speak to us yourself and we will listen but do not let God speak to us, or we will die." I made several trips up and down the mountain to talk with God. With each trip, I gained more and more insight into what God expected of us. One such trip was VERY interesting and lasted 40days and nights. Joshua walked with me part of the way up the mountain, and we had a pretty good talk during the walk. I proceeded the rest of the way alone. When I went up on the mountain, the cloud covered it, and the glory of the LORD settled on Mount Sinai. The sight of the glory of the LORD was like a consuming fire on the mountaintop in the eyes of the Israelites. The Lord told me that we were to build a tabernacle, so that He may dwell with us. The specifics of the tabernacle are a bit much for this discussion, but trust me when I tell you His instructions were very specific. He gave me everything from the dimensions of it to the layout, to the things that are to go into it. He even had specifics instructions on who could enter into different areas of the tabernacle and the consequences of not following His instructions. There were even instructions on how to dress when entering into the tabernacle. He also told of the sacrifices, what would be sacrificed, how to prepare the sacrifice, who would offer the sacrifice. Again, everything was very specific and the consequences for not doing as instructed were equally specific.

Then the LORD said to me, "Go down at once! For your people, whom you brought up out of the land of Egypt have corrupted themselves. How quickly they have turned aside from the way I commanded them. They have made for themselves a molten calf and have bowed down to it. They have sacrificed to it and said, 'O Israel, this is your God, who brought you up out of the land of Egypt.'" He continued to say, "I have seen these people, and they are indeed a stiff-necked people. Now leave Me alone, so that My anger may burn against them and consume them. Then I will make you into a great nation." At first, I just shook my head in disbelief, and then I realized that God really did intend to wipe them out. I entreated the LORD, saying, "O LORD, why are you so angry with Your people, whom You brought out of Egypt with great power and a mighty hand? Why should the Egyptians declare, 'He brought them out with evil intent, to kill them in the mountains and wipe them from the face of the earth'? Turn from Your fierce anger and relent from harming Your people. Remember Your servants Abraham, Isaac, and Israel, to whom You swore, 'I will make your descendants as numerous as the stars in the sky, and I will give your descendants all this land that I have promised, and it shall be their inheritance forever.'" So, God changed His mind and decided not to wipe them out. I turned and went down the mountain with the two tablets of the Testimony in my hands. They were inscribed on both sides. The tablets were the work of God, and the writing was the writing of God. When Joshua saw me coming down the mountain, he said, "The sound of war is in the camp." I replied: "It is neither the cry of victory nor the cry of defeat; I hear the sound of singing!"

When we approached the camp and saw the calf and the dancing, I was furious and threw the tablets, smashing them at the base of the mountain. I took the calf they had made, burned it in the fire, ground it to powder, and scattered the powder over the water. Then I forced the congregation to drink it. After that, I confronted Aaron. "What did these people do to make you lead them into so great a sin?" Aaron began to justify his actions saying, "Don't be angry, you know the people are intent on evil. They told me, 'Make us gods who will go before us. As for this Moses who brought us up out of the land of Egypt, we do not know what has happened to him!" So, I stood at the entrance of the camp and said, "Whoever is for the LORD, come to me." All the Levites gathered around me. "This is what the LORD, says: 'Each of you men is to fasten his sword to his side, go back and forth through the camp from gate to gate, and slay his brother, friend, and neighbor.'" The Levites did so, and about 3000 people died that day. Afterward, I said, "Today you have been ordained for service to the LORD since each man went against his son and his brother; so He has bestowed a blessing on you this day." The next day, early in the morning I said to the people, "You have committed a great sin. Now I will go up to the LORD, maybe I can make atonement for your sin." I returned to the LORD and said, "Oh, what a great sin these people have committed; they have made gods of gold for themselves. Yet now, if You would only forgive their sin. If not, please erase me out of the book that You have written also." The LORD replied, "Whoever has sinned against Me, I will wipe out of My book. Now go, lead the people to the place I told you. My angel shall go before you, but on the day I settle accounts, I will punish them for their sin." Then the LORD said, "Chisel out two stone tablets like the original ones, and I will write on them the words that were on the first tablets, which you broke. I bowed down to the ground and worshiped. "O Lord," I said, "if I have indeed found favor in Your sight, my Lord, please go with us; although, this is a stiff-necked people, forgive our iniquity and sin, and take us as Your inheritance."

The LORD said, "Behold, I am making a covenant. Before

all your people I will perform wonders that have never been done in any nation in all the world. All the people among whom you live will see the LORD's work, for it is an awesome thing that I am doing with you. Observe what I command you this day. I will drive out before you the Amorites, Canaanites, Hittites, Perizzites, Hivites, and Jebusites. Be careful not to make a treaty with the inhabitants of the land you are entering, lest they become a snare in your midst. You must tear down their altars, smash their sacred stones, and chop down their Asherah poles. For you must not worship any other god, for the LORD, whose name is Jealous, is a jealous God. Do not make a covenant with the inhabitants of the land. For when they prostitute themselves to their gods and sacrifice to them, they will invite you, and you will eat their sacrifices. When you take some of their daughters as brides for your sons, their daughters will prostitute themselves to their gods and cause your sons to do the same. Six days you shall labor, but on the seventh day you shall rest; even in the seasons of plowing and harvesting, you must rest. The LORD also said, "Write down these words, for in them I have made a covenant with you and with Israel." I was there with the LORD forty days and forty nights without eating bread or drinking water. He wrote on the tablets the words of the covenant, the Ten Commandments When I came down from Mount Sinai with the two tablets of the Testimony in my hands, I was unaware that my face had become radiant from speaking with the LORD. Aaron and the people looked at me, and they were afraid to approach me. I called out to them; so Aaron and all the leaders of the congregation came to me, and I spoke to them. I commanded them to do everything that the LORD had told me on Mount Sinai. When I had finished speaking to them, I put a veil over my face.

On the twentieth day of the second month of the second year, the cloud was lifted from above the Tabernacle of the Testimony; it was time to move. We set out from the

Wilderness of Sinai, traveling from place to place with the ark of the covenant in front of us until the cloud settled in the Wilderness of Paran. It turned out to be a three-day journey, and along the way, whenever the ark was lifted, I would say, ""Rise up, O LORD! May Your enemies be scattered; may those who hate You flee before You." When it came to rest, I would say: "Return, O LORD, to the countless thousands of Israel." Soon the people began to complain again, and when the Lord heard them, He was very angry, and fire of the LORD burned among them and consumed the outskirts of the camp. The people cried out to me, and I prayed to the LORD, and the fire died down. That place was called Taberah because the fire of the LORD had burned among them.

This is a group of hard-headed people. Not long after seeing people consumed by the fire of the Lord, because of their complaining, the mixed multitude among them had a strong craving for other food, and again the Israelites wept and said, "Who will feed us meat? So, I asked the LORD, "Why have You brought this trouble on Your servant? Why have I not found favor in Your sight, that You have laid upon me the burden of all these people? I cannot carry all these people by myself; it is too oppressive for me. If this is how You are going to treat me, please kill me right now, if I have found favor in Your eyes, and let me not see my misery." I thought to myself, "Let me die?" Before I realized it, that complaining spirit had jumped on me, and I was sounding like everyone else. Then the LORD said to me, "Bring Me seventy of the elders of Israel known to you as leaders and officers of the people. Bring them to the Tent of Meeting and have them stand there with you. I will come down and speak with you there, and I will take some of the Spirit that is on you and put that Spirit upon them. They will help you bear the burden of the people so that you do not have to bear it by yourself." I guess through all the complaining, I had forgotten, that Jethro had suggested this very thing to me a little over a month ago.

Then the Lord said, say to the people: "Consecrate yourselves for tomorrow, and you will eat meat, because you have cried out, saying, 'Who will feed us meat? We were better off in Egypt.' Therefore, the LORD will give you meat, and you will eat. You will eat meat for a whole month until it comes out of your nostrils and makes you nauseous.'" Later, a wind sent by the LORD came up, drove in quail from the sea, and dropped them near the camp, about two cubits deep for a day's journey in every direction around the camp. For two days, the people stayed up gathering the quail. No one gathered less than ten homers, and they spread them out all around the camp. While the meat was still between their teeth, before it was chewed, the LORD's anger burned against the people, and the LORD struck them with a severe plague, and they called that place Kibroth-hattaavah, because they buried the people who had craved meat. We left Kibroth-hattaavah and moved to Hazeroth, where we remained for a while.

Evidently, the desert heat must be making people crazy. Now Miriam and Aaron are complaining about me marrying a Cushite woman. "Does the LORD speak only through Moses?" they said. "Does He not also speak through us?" The LORD heard this, and suddenly the LORD said to me, Aaron, and Miriam, "You three, come out to the Tent of Meeting." We went out, and the LORD came down in a pillar of cloud, stood at the entrance to the Tent, and summoned Aaron and Miriam. Both of them stepped forward. He said, "Hear now My words. If there is a prophet among you, I will reveal Myself to him in a vision. I will speak to him in a dream. This was not so with My servant Moses; he is faithful in all My house. I speak with him face to face, clearly and not in riddles; he sees the form of the LORD. Why then were you not afraid to speak against him?" The LORD got very angry at them, and He departed. As the cloud lifted from above the Tent, suddenly Miriam became leprous, white as snow. Aaron turned toward her, saw that she was leprous, and said to me, "Please do not hold this sin against us that we have so foolishly committed. So, I cried out to the LORD, "O God, please heal her!" The LORD answered me, "If her father had spit in her face, would she not have been disgraced for seven days? Let her be confined outside the camp for seven days; after that, she may come back in." After seven days Miriam rejoined the camp, and we journeyed from Hazeroth to Paran.

When the camp was completely set up, the Lord said to me, "Send men to spy out the land of Canaan, which I am giving to you. One man, who is a leader from each tribe will go." I told them, "Go up through the Negev and into the hill country. See what the land is like and whether its people are strong or weak, few or many. Is the land where they live good or bad? Are the cities where they dwell open camps or fortified? Be courageous, and bring back some of the fruit of the land." They went and spied out the land from the wilderness of Zin as far as Rehob, toward Lebo-hamath. They went through the Negev and came to Hebron, where Ahiman, Sheshai, and Talmai, the descendants of Anak, dwelled. It had been built seven years before Zoan in Egypt. When they came to the Valley of Eshcol, they cut down a branch with a single cluster of grapes, which they carried on a pole between two men. They also took some pomegranates and figs. When they returned, they gave this account to me: "We went into the land to which you sent us, and indeed, it is flowing with milk and honey. Here is some of its fruit! However, the people living in the land are strong, and the cities are large and fortified. We even saw the descendants of Anak there. The Amalekites live in the land of the Negev; the Hittites, Jebusites, and Amorites live in the hill country; and the Canaanites live by the sea and along the Jordan."

Then Caleb quieted the people and said, "We must go up and take possession of the land, for we can certainly conquer it!" However, the men who had gone with him replied, "We cannot go up against the people, for they are stronger than we are! We seemed like grasshoppers in our sight, and we must have seemed the same to them!" Then all the Israelites murmured against me and Aaron, and everyone said, "If only we had died in the land of Egypt, or if only we had died in this wilderness! Why is the LORD bringing us into this land to be killed by the sword? Let us appoint a leader and return to Egypt." Remember when I said be careful who you hang around, and evil communications, corrupt good manners? What was so special about Egypt that they kept wanting to return to? For the mixed multitude, it was home. The Egyptians in the group had a great life, that they saw crumble in the hands of an Almighty God. The slaves didn't fare too badly because they were hated by the Egyptians. The Hebrews, on the other hand, were despised and treated cruelly. Be careful who you let influence your decisions and actions. You may find yourself worse off than you were before.

Joshua son of Nun and Caleb son of Jephunneh, who were among those who had spied out the land, tore their clothes and said, "The land we passed through and explored is exceedingly good. If the LORD delights in us, He will bring us into this land, a land flowing with milk and honey, and He will give it to us. Do not rebel against the LORD, and do not be afraid of the people of the land, for they will be like bread for us. Their protection has been removed, and the LORD is with us. Do not be afraid of them!" Aaron and I fell to the ground, facedown, as the congregation threatened to stone Joshua and Caleb. Then the glory of the LORD appeared to all the Israelites at the Tent of Meeting. The LORD said, "How long will these people treat Me with contempt? How long will they refuse to believe in Me, despite all the signs I have performed among them? I will strike them with a plague and destroy them, and I will make you into a nation greater and mightier than they are."

I replied, "LORD, the Egyptians will hear of it, for by Your strength You brought these people from among them. They will tell it to the inhabitants of this land. They have already heard that You are in the midst of this people, and, have been seen face to face. Your cloud stands over them, and that You go before them in a pillar of cloud by day and a pillar of fire by night. If You kill these people as one man, the nations who have heard of Your fame will say, 'Because the LORD was unable to bring these people into the land He swore to give them, He has slaughtered them in the wilderness.' So now I pray, may the power of the Lord be magnified, just as You have declared: 'The LORD is slow to anger and abounding in loving devotion, forgiving wrongdoing and rebellion. But He will by no means leave the guilty unpunished. Pardon the iniquity of this people, in keeping with the greatness of Your loving devotion."

"I have pardoned them as you requested," the LORD replied. "Yet as surely as I live and the earth is filled with My glory, not one of the men who have seen My glory and the signs I performed in Egypt and the wilderness will ever see the land I swore to give their fathers. None of those who have treated Me with contempt and disobeyed Me will see it. Everyone twenty years of age or older will die in the wilderness because you have grumbled against Me. Nevertheless, my servants Joshua and Caleb have a different spirit and have followed Me wholeheartedly. I will bring them into the land they have entered, and their descendants will inherit it. Now since the Amalekites and Canaanites are living in the valleys, turn back tomorrow and head for the wilderness along the route to the Red Sea. Your children will be shepherds in the wilderness for forty years, and they will suffer for your unfaithfulness." Then, the men that spied out the land, and who had spread the bad report about the land were struck down by a plague before the LORD, and all the Israelites mourned bitterly.

Now if you're under the impression that I'm leading a group of hard-headed people, you would be correct, and it's about to get worse. The following morning, some of the people, decided they were going to head to the land promised by God. I urged them not to go because God would not be with them. They went anyway and died at the hands of the Amalekites and Canaanites. Next, Korah, Dathan, and Abiram, along with 250 leaders of the congregation started a rebellion. They railed, "Who are you to rule over us?" I replied to the whole congregation. "Separate yourselves from these men and everything that pertains to them. This is how you will know that the LORD has sent me to do all these things. If these men die a natural death, or if they suffer the fate of all men, then the LORD has not sent me. However, if the LORD does a new thing, and the Earth opens up and swallows them and everything that belongs to them, then you will know that these men have treated the LORD with contempt." As soon as I finished speaking, the ground opened up and swallowed them and their families also. Then fire came from heaven and consumed the 250 men that stood with them. The next day the entire congregation of Israel grumbled against me and Aaron, saying, "You have killed the LORD's people!" Suddenly the cloud covered the Tent of Meeting and the glory of the LORD appeared. We went to the front of the Tent of Meeting, and the LORD said, "Get away from this congregation so that I may consume them in an instant." I said to Aaron, "Take your censer, place fire from the altar in it, and add incense. Go quickly to the congregation and make atonement for them, because wrath has gone out from the LORD, and the plague has begun." Aaron did as commanded, and stood between the living and the dead, and the plague stopped. An additional 14,700 people died there.

Next, we traveled to the Wilderness of Zin and stayed in Kadesh. There Miriam died and was buried. There was no water for the people, so they gathered against me and Aaron. They said, "If only we had perished when our brothers fell dead before the LORD! I'm about sick of these people. They haven't learned a thing! God showed Himself faithful, miraculous, and merciful, time and again. Yet, at the first sign of adversity, all they can do is complain! We went to the entrance of the Tent of Meeting and bowed down. The glory of the LORD appeared to us. The LORD said, "Assemble the people and speak to the rock in their presence, and water will pour out of it." I assembled the people and said, "Listen now, you rebels; must we bring you water out of this rock?" In my frustration with the people I struck the rock twice with my staff, and water gushed out. The LORD said to me and Aaron, "Because you did not trust Me to show My holiness in the sight of the Israelites, you will not bring this assembly into the land I have given them."

Sorrowfully (at least for me anyway), we traveled to Mount Hor near the border of Edom. The Lord said, "Aaron will be taken from his people; he will not enter the land I have given the Israelites, because both of you rebelled against My command at the waters of Meribah. Take Aaron and his son Eleazar and bring them up to Mount Hor. Remove Aaron's priestly garments and put them on his son Eleazar. Aaron died there on top of the mountain. Then Eleazar and I came down from the mountain with me. When all the congregation saw that Aaron had died, they mourned him for thirty days.

After leaving Mount Hor we traveled along the Red Sea to avoid Edom, and as you can probably guess, the people grew impatient and began to complain AGAIN. They spoke out against God and me. "Why have you led us up out of Egypt to die in the wilderness? There is no bread or water, and we hate this light bread." So, the LORD sent poisonous snakes among the people, and many of the Israelites were bitten and died. Then the people came to me and said, "We have sinned by speaking against the LORD and you. Intercede with the LORD to take the snakes away from us." So, I interceded for the people, and the LORD said,

"Make a snake and mount it on a pole. When anyone who is bitten looks at it, he will live." As I am fashioning this snake of bronze, all I could think about was, will they ever learn? They complain, God provides; they complain louder, God provides a punishment; they complain to the point of rebellion, God provides death. How many people must suffer or die before they learn their lesson? I finished the bronze snake and mounted it on a pole. Everyone who was bitten, and looked at the serpent, recovered.

I fear my journey is quickly coming to its expected end. There are only three of us left since we were told no one over 20 would enter into the promised land. Unfortunately, I will not be entering the promised land either. I can't believe I allowed all that complaining to get to me; especially to the point where it would cause me to disobey God's command. I tried again to convince God to let me enter into the promised land. None of my arguments/ reasonings would work. Not even reminding Him of all the times I was able to intercede for those knuckleheads and kept them from getting completely wiped out. HA! I was even desperate enough to try a little flattery. I said' "O Lord GOD, You have begun to show Your greatness and power to Your servant. For what god in heaven or on earth can perform such works and mighty acts as Yours? Please let me cross over and see the beautiful land beyond the Jordan, that wonderful hill country and Lebanon!" The Lord got angry with me and said, "That is enough, do not speak to Me again about this matter." It wouldn't be until much later that anyone would learn the significance of speaking to that rock instead of striking it a second time. So, I guess the wise thing to do would be to find a successor to lead these people into the promised land. I petitioned God, and Joshua was chosen to lead the congregation into the promised land.

I gave one last exhortation for obedience to the Lord. I am teaching you to follow His law, so that you may live.

Enter and take possession of the land that the LORD is giving you. You must not add to or subtract from what I command you, so that you may keep the commandments of the LORD your God. Your eyes have seen what the LORD did at Baal-peor. He destroyed from among you all who followed Baal, but you who held fast to the LORD are alive to this day. I have taught you statutes and ordinances just as the LORD my God has commanded me, so that you may follow them in the land you are about to enter and possess. Observe them carefully, for this will show your understanding and wisdom in the sight of the peoples, who shall hear of all these statutes and say, "Surely this great nation is a wise and understanding people." Be on your guard and diligently watch yourselves, so that you do not forget the things your eyes have seen, and so that they do not slip from your heart as long as you live. Teach them to your children and grandchildren. Hear, O Israel: The LORD our God, the LORD is One. And you shall love the LORD your God with all your heart and with all your soul and with all your strength.

Then I went up from the plains of Moab to Mount Nebo, to the top of Pisgah, which faces Jericho, and the LORD showed me the whole land. The LORD said, "This is the land I swore to give Abraham, Isaac, and Jacob, when I said, 'I will give it to your descendants.' I have let you see it with your own eyes, but you will not cross into it." My 120-year journey has come to its end. I died there in the land of Moab, and the Lord buried me in a valley in the land of Moab facing Beth-peor, and no one to this day knows the location of my grave. No prophet has arisen in Israel like me since that time, whom the LORD knew face to face.

Samson: Greatness in the Face of Tragedy

You've all heard the saying, 'You play with fire, and you will get burned.' I can attest that it is true. My name is Samson, and people think I'm just a dumb brute. I guess I am to blame for that because, in retrospect, I made some pretty dumb decisions. However, don't think that's all there is to me. I was judge over Israel for 20 years and I was ordained by God to begin Israel's deliverance from the Philistines. So let's get into my story.

It all began with Israel being a "hot mess". To say sin was running rampant in Israel would be an understatement. It is said that Israel did EVIL in the sight of the Lord. As a result, the Lord delivered them into captivity to the Philistines for forty years. Now Manoah, a Danite, had a barren wife, and the Angel of the LORD appeared to the woman and said to her, "Is it true that you are barren and have no children? You will conceive and give birth to a son. You must not drink wine or strong drink, and cannot eat anything unclean. A razor cannot come over his head, because the boy will be a Nazirite; set apart to God from the womb. He will begin the deliverance of Israel from the hands of the Philistines." After she told these things to Manoah, her husband, he prayed to the LORD, "Please, O Lord, let the Man of God You sent us; come to us again to teach us how to raise the boy who is to be born." (Judges 13:8) God heard the voice of Manoah, and the Angel of God returned to the woman as she was sitting in the field. She ran to her husband and said, "The Man who came to me the other day has reappeared". So, Manoah got up and followed her back to the field. When he came to the Man, he asked, "Are You the Man who spoke to my wife?" "I am," He said. Then Manoah asked, "When Your words come to pass, what will be the boy's purpose in life." Then the Angel of the LORD answered Manoah, "Your wife needs to do everything I told her. She is not to eat anything that comes from the vine nor drink wine or strong drink. She must not eat anything unclean. Your wife must do everything I have commanded her." After hearing these things Manoah said to the Angel of the LORD, "Please stay here and we will prepare a young goat for you." The Angel of the LORD replied, "Even if I stay, I will not eat your food, but if you prepare a burnt offering, offer it to the LORD." Then Manoah said to Him, "What is Your name, so that we may honor You when Your words come to pass?" "Why do you ask My name," asked the Angel, "since it is beyond comprehension?"

Then Manoah took a young goat and a grain offering and offered them on a rock to the LORD. As he and his wife looked on, the LORD did a spectacular thing. When the flame went up from the altar to the sky, the Angel of the LORD ascended in the flame. When they saw this, they fell facedown to the ground. When the Angel of the LORD did not appear again to them, Manoah realized that it was the Angel of the LORD. According to the time of life; the woman gave birth to a son and named me Samson. I grew, and the LORD blessed me.

One day I went down to Timnah, where I saw a young Philistine woman. Later that day, I returned and told my father and mother, "I have seen a woman of the Philistines in Timnah. Now get her for me as a wife." My father and mother replied, "Can you not find a young woman among any of our people? Why must you go to the uncircumcised Philistines to get a wife?" I told my father, "Get her for me, for she is pleasing to me." (Now his father and mother did not know this was from the LORD, who was seeking an occasion to move against the Philistines; for at that time the Philistines were ruling over Israel. Judges 14: 4) I went down to Timnah with my father and mother and came to the vineyards of Timnah. Suddenly a young lion came roaring at me. The Spirit of the LORD took control of me, and I tore the lion apart with my bare hands, but I did not tell my father or mother what I had done. I continued on my way to the city and spoke to the woman because I wanted her. When I returned home; I noticed the lion's carcass on the side of the road. In it was a swarm of bees, along with their honey. I scooped some honey into my hands and ate it as I continued home. When I reached my father and mother, I gave some to them and they ate it. However, I did not tell them that I had taken the honey from the lion's carcass.

Now, remember my opening statement? This was my first bout with the fire. I knew I wasn't supposed to touch that lion, but I did because I wanted some honey. What should have happened is this: he shall not go near a dead body. He shall not make himself unclean even for his father or his mother, for his brother or his sister, when they die, because his separation to God is on his head. All the days of his separation he shall be holy to the LORD. (Numbers 6: 6-8) This is most likely because separation from death (the effect of sin) was essential during the period of the vow.

Then my father went to visit the woman, and I prepared a feast there, as was customary for the bridegroom. When the Philistines saw me, they selected thirty men to accompany me. As the men, followed me I said to them "Let me tell you a riddle. If you can solve it for me within the seven days of the feast, I will give you thirty linen garments and thirty sets of clothes, but if you cannot solve it, you must give me thirty linen garments and thirty sets of clothes." "Tell us your riddle," they replied. Confidently, I said to them: "Out of the eater came something to eat, and out of the strong came something sweet." For three days they were unable to solve the riddle. Frustrated with their inability to solve the riddle; on the fourth day, they said to my wife, "Did you invite us here to rob us? Convince your husband to explain the riddle to us. If not, we will burn you and your father's household to death." Then my wife came to me, weeping, and said, "Why do you hate me? You do not truly love me! You have posed a riddle to my people, but have not explained it to me." I replied, "I have not even explained it to my parents, so why should I explain it to you?" She whined and complained the rest days of the feast, and finally, on the seventh day, I told her the answer. She then explained the riddle to her people. Before sunset on the seventh day, the men of the city said to me: "What is sweeter than honey? What is stronger than a lion?"

Upset that they answered the riddle, I said to them: "If you had not asked with my heifer, you would not have been able to solve my riddle!" Then the Spirit of the LORD came upon me mightily, and I went down to Ashkelon; I killed thirty of their men and took their clothes. I gave their clothes to those who had solved the riddle. This is the second time that I have essentially broken my vow by touching something that was dead. I returned to my father's house infuriated. At the time of the wheat harvest; I took a young goat and went to visit my wife. "I want to go to my wife in her room," I said, but her father would not let me in. He said, "I was sure you hated her, so I gave her to one of the men who accompanied you. Her younger sister is even more beautiful than she is. Please take her instead." I said to him, "This time I will be blameless in harming the Philistines."

I went out and caught three hundred foxes, and gathered torches. I turned the foxes tail-to-tail and tied a torch between each pair of tails. Then I lit the torches and released the foxes into the standing grain of the Philistines. The fire blazed out of control; burning up the piles of grain and the standing grain, as well as the vineyards and olive groves. "Who did this?" the Philistines leaders demanded. A man responded, "It was Samson, the son-in-law of the Timnite. Her father gave his wife to one of his friends." So, the Philistines burned her and her father to death. When I found out what happened, I told them, "Because you have done this, I will not rest until I have taken vengeance upon you." I struck them brutally with a great slaughter and then went to stay in the cave at the rock of Etam.

The following day; three thousand men of Judah came to the cave, and asked me, "Have you forgotten that the Philistines rule over us? What have you done to us? The Philistines have encamped in Judah, and demanded your arrest." "I have slaughtered them; like they slaughtered my wife and father-in-law"; I replied. They said to me, "We have come down to arrest you and hand you over to the Philistines." I said, "Swear to me that you will not kill me yourselves and I will go with you." "No, we will not kill you. We will bind you securely and hand you over to them", they replied. So, they bound me with two new ropes and led me up from the cave. When I arrived in Lehi, the Philistines came out shouting against me. Then the Spirit of the LORD came upon me and the ropes on my arms became like burnt flax. The bonds broke loose from my hands, and I found the fresh jawbone of a donkey. I reached out my hand and grabbed it. I mercilessly slew a thousand men, and said, "With the jawbone of a donkey I have piled them up. With the jawbone of a donkey I have slain them." When I had finished speaking, I cast the jawbone from my hand; and I named that place Ramath-lehi (height of a jawbone).

Now that was the third strike. I'm not sure what to think about this. I have broken my vow three times, yet the Lord still uses me. How is this possible? Afterward, I was very thirsty, and I cried out to the LORD, "You have accomplished this great deliverance through Your servant. Must I die of thirst now and fall into the hands of the uncircumcised?" God heard my cry and opened up the mortar in Lehi, and water came out of it. I drank some water; my strength returned, and I was revived. I named that place En-hakkore (spring of the one calling), and it remains in Lehi to this day.

One day I went to Gaza, where I saw a prostitute and went in to spend the night with her. When the Gazites heard that I was there; they surrounded that place and lay in wait for me all night. They spoke among themselves saying, "Let us wait until dawn; then we will kill him." I laid there until midnight. Then I got up and took hold of the doors of the city gate, along with the two gateposts, and pulled them out, bars and all. I put them on my shoulders and ran to the top of the mountain overlooking Hebron. Imagine the horror and the embarrassment the Philistines must have felt. To see their mortal enemy run uphill; carrying a ten-ton gate for a little over 30 miles; then planting on the hill for all of Israel to see.

Sometime later, I fell in love with a woman in the Valley of Sorek, named Delilah. We spent a lot of time together. So much so that I neglected my duties as judge over Israel. She made me happier than I had been in a while. One day, Delilah said to me, "Please tell me the source of your great strength and how you could be tied up and subdued." Now you would think; I would have learned my lesson dealing with my late wife. Undoubtedly, I had not. Going against conventional wisdom; I decided to play this game again. I told her, "If they tie me up with seven fresh bowstrings that have not been dried; I will become as weak as any other man." Later that day; the lords of the Philistines brought her seven fresh bowstrings that had not been dried, and she bound me with them. Delilah called out, Samson, the Philistines are here for you." I rose and broke the strings that bound me. Then Delilah said, "You have mocked me and lied to me! Will you now please tell me how you can be bound?" I replied, "If they tie me up with new ropes that have never been used, I will become as weak as any other man." Later that day; Delilah took new ropes; tied me up, and called out, "Samson, the Philistines are here!" While the men were hidden in her room, I snapped the ropes off my arms like a thread. Then Delilah said, "You have mocked me and lied to me all along! Tell me how you can be tied up." I told her, "If you weave the seven braids of my head into the web of a loom and fasten it with a pin, I will become as weak as any other man." While I slept, Delilah took the seven braids of my hair and wove them into the web. Then she fastened the braids with a pin and called to me, "Samson, the Philistines are here!" I awoke from my sleep and pulled out the pin with the loom and the web.

At this point in time, I'm not sure what's worse; my willingness to play this game, or the persistence of the Philistines. On one hand, I've willingly sinned against God. I've lied; fornicated; broken my vow, and married a woman from an uncircumcised people. I know I should not be tempting God like this, but the fact that He had not punished me, had me thinking that I was above His law. On the other hand, you have the Philistines who have seen me kill men with my bare hands; kill 1000 men with a jawbone; carry a gate (approx. 10 tons) on my shoulders and run with it for about 36 miles, and most recently witnessed me lie about the source of my strength and snap bonds like string. Their hatred for me has them completely blinded them, and they will stop at nothing. But I digress.

Frustrated and upset, Delilah said to me, "How can you say, 'I love you' when your heart is not with me? This is the third time you have mocked me and failed to reveal to me the source of your great strength!" Finally, after her continuous nagging and pleading, I was sick of hearing it. I told her everything. "My hair has never been shaven because I have been a Nazirite to God from my mother's womb. If I am shaved, my strength will leave me, and I will become as weak as any other man." The following night, she lulled me to sleep on her lap, she called a man to shave off the seven braids on my head. She began to bind me, and my strength left me. Then she called out, "Samson, the Philistines are here!" When I awoke from my sleep, I thought, "I will shake myself free and escape as I did before", because I did not know that the LORD had departed from me. Finally, the price of my sin has come due. Then the Philistines seized me and gouged out my eyes. They brought me down to Gaza. I was bound with bronze shackles and forced to grind grain in the prison. What a hefty price to pay. However, the hair of my head had begun to grow back after it had been shaved. Having realized the error of my ways, I repented of my folly before the Lord.

Now the lords of the Philistines gathered together to offer a great sacrifice to their god Dagon. They rejoiced and said, "Our god has delivered Samson our enemy into our hands: our enemy who destroyed our land and multiplied our dead." While their hearts were merry, they said, "Call for Samson to entertain us." So, they called me out of the prison to entertain them. They placed me between the pillars. I said to the servant who held my hand, "Lead me where I can feel the pillars that support the temple, so I can lean against them." Now the temple was full of men and women. All the lords of the Philistines were there, with about three thousand men and women who were on the roof watching me entertain them. Then I called out to the LORD: "O Lord GOD, please remember me. Strengthen me, O God, just one more time. With one vengeful blow allow me to pay back the Philistines for my two eyes." I reached out for the two central pillars supporting the temple. Bracing myself against them, with my right hand on one and my left hand on the other, I said, "Let me die with the Philistines." Then I pushed with all my might and the temple fell on the lords and all the people in it. So in my death, I killed more than I had killed in my life, and God set in motion His plan to deliver Israel from the oppression of the Philistines.

David: Delve Into Complicated

Seek and you shall find; although, sometimes you may not like what you find. Never judge a book by its cover, because some things certainly aren't what they appear to be.

For all intents and purposes, I appear to be a lowly shepherd. However, I promise you there's so much more buried deep inside just waiting to get out. Sometimes when I'm out on the hillside; I imagine what it would be like to be more than a shepherd. What if I were a soldier like three of my brothers. Or maybe; to be known as more than just one Jesse's boys. Don't get me wrong; I know that protecting my father's flock is an important job. I love doing my part for the family; it's just that I feel God has bigger plans for me. What can I say? When you're watching animals roam and graze; you have a lot of time to contemplate life. Not to mention; plenty of time to develop a skill or two. Like playing the harp and using a sling. I must say; I'm very good at both (in my opinion).

One day while out in the pasture I spotted a lion headed for the sheep; I hesitated for a slight moment and wonder how I'm going to save the flock. The lion snatched up a sheep into its mouth, and suddenly the Spirit of the Lord quickened my mind. I sprang into action. With God's help, I slew the lion. There also came an occasion that I slew a bear. These are just of few experiences that would inspire me to pen Psalms 63: "O God, thou art my God; early will I seek thee. My soul thirsteth for thee; my flesh longeth for thee in a dry and thirsty land, where no water is..."

One day Samuel came to visit. He requested to see all of

my father's sons. The baffling thing is; no one thought of me. Father introduced his sons to Samuel. First was his oldest son, Eliab. Eliab impressed Samuel greatly. He was both strong and tall. Samuel's first thought was; such an impressive young man would be a good king. However, Samuel was wrong. God explained to Samuel. "When people choose a leader; they often select an impressive or powerful man. They make the decision based on what they can see. However, I see what people cannot. I know what's in a person's heart. That person's true thoughts and attitudes". When God chooses a leader; that person may not seem impressive. However, God will give that person the skills that he will need for the task. God did not choose Eliab. He did not choose Abinadab (my second brother) or Shammah (my third brother) either. In fact, God did not choose any of my six brothers introduced to him. Now Samuel was puzzled because he was certain that he knew what God wanted. So he inquired of my father; "Are these all your sons?" My father replied, "My youngest son, David, is in the field tending the sheep." Samuel immediately requested my presence. When I arrived to meet Samuel; he had this look of shock on his face. Clearly; I wasn't who; or what he expected. However, Samuel knew that I was what God expected. He took out his horn of oil and anointed me king of Israel. Now Saul was still on the throne so I had to wait for this to come to pass. I, however, understood the importance of this moment. The presence of God rested upon me and it confirmed something I had always felt. God had something special in store for me.

As time passed an old enemy prepared for war. The Philistines had entered the valley of Elah. Saul sent out only his best soldiers to meet them. For 40 days they looked across the valley at each other. For 40 days the Philistine champion came out to intimidate them saying "Send me a man so that I can fight with him. If he wins, we shall be your servants. If I win; you shall be ours." One day I was sent to the front line with food for my brothers. As I was talking with them, I could hear this loud voice crying out "Send me a man…". I went out to see who it was. There stood this giant of a man, 10 ft. tall (well more like 6 cubits and a span, but since no one is sure exactly how long a span is, I'm making him 10 ft.). Now his armor was equally impressive (1 Samuel 17:5-7). As I looked around; I could see the fear that gripped the army of the Lord. Something began to well-up within me. Word began circulating around the camp; any man who would fight against Goliath and win could marry the king's daughter. She was beautiful, so the offer was quite tempting. As I began to confirm this story; Eliab must have gotten jealous because he scolded me for being there. Word got back to Saul of my inquiry, and he called me to his tent. When I entered Saul's tent I said, "Don't worry about this uncircumcised Philistine, I will fight him and defeat him." Saul smirked. "You're just a boy; what makes you so sure you can beat him?" I said, "I have killed lions and bears. This uncircumcised Philistine will suffer the same fate because he has defied the army of the Lord." Saul called his armor-bearer to bring his armor. Needless to say; it was too big and awkward. I graciously declined to wear the king's armor because it was unproven to me. I went out into the valley to face Goliath armed only with my staff, my sling, and five smooth stones.

When Goliath saw me, he mocked me saying, "Am I a dog; that you come to me with a stick?" Then he cursed me by his gods. This uncircumcised Philistine has NO idea who he is talking to. Then I said to Goliath, "You come to me with a sword, a spear, and a javelin. I come to you in the name of the LORD of hosts; the God of the armies of Israel; whom you have taunted. Today, the Lord will deliver you into my hands. I will strike you down and remove your head from your body. I will give the dead bodies of your army to the birds of the sky, and to the wild beast of the Earth. Then will all the Earth know that there is a God in Israel and that all this assembly may know that the LORD does not deliver by the sword or spear. The battle is the LORD'S, and He will give you into our hands." So, I slew Goliath, the Philistines were defeated and we returned to Jerusalem with the spoils.

Goliath and the Philistines have been defeated; Jonathan (Saul's son) and I became best friends; I've been made a part of Saul's court. I would play my harp to soothe Saul whenever an evil spirit came upon him. I've been put over part of the army, and what do I get for my service to the king, jealousy and a spear thrown at me! Later Saul sent me out to battle time and time again. Each time; hoping that the Philistines would kill me. Nevertheless, the Lord was with me, and everything I touched prospered. After it became apparent to Saul that the Philistines could not defeat us; Saul ordered Jonathan and his men to kill me. Jonathan warned me of Saul's plot, and I returned to my father's house. Meanwhile, Jonathan talked Saul into changing his mind. Later I returned to the palace believing that Saul had made peace within himself, and continued my duties. I also inherited greater responsibilities. Not only did I become his armor-bearer, but I also became his bodyguard. Saul continued to send me out to battle the Philistines and each subsequent victory was greater than the previous one.

HA! You would think that Saul would be happy that we are constantly defeating his greatest enemy. Not the case; the more battles we won; the more jealous he got. So once again; an evil spirit came upon Saul, and once again I played my harp, and for the second time I found myself dodging his spear. I ran back to my home. Later that day my wife (Michal) told me of a plot that her father has come up with to have me killed. She lowers me down from the window and dressed the statue in our house to look like a man lying in the bed. When Saul's messenger came to the house, Michal lied to them to protect me. I fled to Ramah and met Samuel. I told him what Saul had done. We then went to Naioth. When Saul heard where I was, he sent men to capture me there. When the men arrived; they saw a group of prophets prophesying. The Spirit of the Lord came upon them, and they began to prophesy. This happened three times; then Saul himself came to kill me. As he approached Naioth; the Spirit of the Lord came upon him, and he began to prophesy. He even stripped off his clothes and laid before Samuel prophesying.

I left Naioth and returned to the palace to see Jonathan. When I saw him, I asked him why his father was trying to kill me. Jonathan replied, "My father does not make a move without me knowing about it. Why do you think he's trying to kill you? I don't know anything about this plan." Then I explained what had happened. Jonathan was shocked, but we reaffirmed our commitment to one another. Later we devised a plan to find out what Saul was up to. The day after the new moon; the second day that my place at the feast was empty; Saul said to Jonathan his son, "Why has the son of Jesse not come to the either yesterday or today? Jonathan answered Saul saying, "David earnestly asked to leave so he could go to Bethlehem. He said, 'Please let me go, since our family has a sacrifice in the city, and my brother has commanded me to attend. If I have found favor in your sight; please let me get away that I may see my brothers.' For this reason; he has not come to the king's table." Then Saul's anger burned against Jonathan. He said to him, "You son of a perverse, rebellious woman! Don't you think I know that you are choosing the son of

Jesse to your shame and the shame of your mother? For as long as the son of Jesse lives on the earth, neither you nor your kingdom will be established. Therefore now, send and bring him to me, for he must surely die." Jonathan answered, "Why should he be put to death? What has he done?" Then Saul hurled his spear at him. So, Jonathan knew that his father had decided to put me to death. Then Jonathan arose from the table in anger and did not eat food on the second day of the new moon, because he was grieved over me, and because his father had dishonored him.

On the third day, as planned, Jonathan came out to the field and shot an arrow. He called out to the boy he had brought with him, "The arrow has PASSED you. GO retrieve it." My heart sinks within me because now I knew I had to run and hide. Jonathan sent the boy back to the palace with his bow and arrows. When he was out of sight, I met Jonathan to say goodbye. A very bitter goodbye it was because I really cherished our friendship. Honestly, it was much deeper than merely a friendship. There was a real bond between us, and as I wept bitterly Jonathan said, "Go in safety; inasmuch, as we have sworn to each other in the name of the LORD, saying, 'The LORD will be between me and you, and between our descendants forever." As I began my life on the run; I had no idea how long this is going to last. I did know God had a plan and I had to trust Him.

Trust God? Sometimes that's easier said than done. Especially at this point. I mean, I'm running for my life right now because I trusted God. Needless to say, I'm having trust issues right about now, and to add insult to injury, I'm headed to Gath. Yes, the same Gath that Goliath was from (in Philistia). It seems like a bad idea to me, but

I'm trying to work through my trust issues. On my way to Gath, I stopped in Nob to see Ahimelech the chief priest. Maybe he would have an idea why God was leading me to Gath. When I met with Ahimelech, he asked me why I was traveling alone, and I kinda lied to him. I told him that the king sent me away on a secret mission. Don't look at me like that, because it was Saul's actions that had me in Nob anyway. So, most of what I said was true, and the rest of it, I can justify it as the truth if you like. Ahimelech gave me some bread and Goliath's sword and I headed off to Gath.

Upon entering Gath, I was recognized by one of king Achish's servants, and I immediately figured I had just jumped out of the fryer, and into the fire. I knew this was a bad idea! How am I going to get myself out of this mess? I know, I'll act like I'm crazy (which at this point isn't really a stretch). So, I began to mark on the doors while drooling and the king bought it. He had me thrown out of the city and I headed to the cave of Adullam; where I was joined by my family and others fleeing Saul's madness. We then journeyed to Mizpah where I asked the king of Moab if my parents could stay there until I figure out what God wanted me to do. After leaving Mizpah, we ran into the prophet Gad who told me not to stay in the stronghold (inaccessible place) but to go to Judah. We obeyed and went to the forest of Hereth. While there, we were joined by Abaithar, who brought us news of the massacre at Nob. Doeg the Edomite, slew all the priest by order of the king. I explained to Abaithar that it was my fault that the priest had been slain. Saul's hatred and jealousy for me had spilled over to anyone who aided me. I convinced Abaithar to remain with me and he'd be safe.

Word came to us that Keilah (a city of Judah on the Israeli-Philistia border) was being attacked by the Philistines.

I inquired of the Lord, should I attack? He replied, "Go attack the Philistines and deliver Keilah". When I told my men of the plans, they were afraid, so I inquired a second time and God replied: "Arise, go down to Keilah, for I will give the Philistines into your hand." We went to Keilah and as promised; we slaughter the Philistines and took their livestock as spoils. Then we settled in Keilah. Now as you would expect; news of the slaughter made it back to Saul and he was furious. He brought an army to Keilah in an attempt to capture me, but my men and I escape and went to Ziph at Horesh. Jonathan met me at Horesh and reaffirmed our covenant (1 Samuel 23:17-18). Just when you think things are settling down, and running is no longer necessary; some of the Ziphites betrayed us and told Saul of our whereabouts. Just when it appeared as though Saul was going to surround us in the wilderness of Maon; a word came to him that the Philistines had attacked and he returned home to defend his kingdom. From Maon, we went to Engedi. While in Engedi, this game of hide-and-seek with Saul began to turn in my favor. I had the chance to kill Saul and choose to cut off the bottom of his robe instead. My men were very disappointed in me and wanted to kill him themselves. I persuaded them not to because Saul is still king of Israel and therefore, still considered God's anointed. It's not our place to deal with Saul; it's God's. When I revealed to Saul what I had done; he wept bitterly, we entered into a covenant and he returned home.

I have just received news that Samuel has died. We went to Ramah to pay our respects. While at Samuel's funeral Saul and I are face-to-face. Surprisingly he has laid his hatred aside long enough to mourn a prophet and dear friend. After the funeral; instead of returning to the caves of Engedi; we went to Maon to find some work. We found employment with one of the richest men in Maon. Nabal had an unbelievably large flock (1 Samuel 25 2-3), and we watched over his flock and shepherds. Shearing time came has arrived, and it's time to get paid. I sent 10 men to Nabal to receive our payment. When my men returned, they brought word; not only of Nabal's refusal to pay but of his insult as well (1 Samuel 25: 9-13). Now there's going to be some bloodshed. I told 400 of my best men to get their weapon and we're going to take what is rightfully ours. Nabal and all the males of his house and servants are going to die. As we approached Nabal's farm we were met by Abigail, Nabal's wife. She asked for permission to speak, and I heard her out. She admitted to Nabal's wrongdoing but asked for mercy. She continued to say that God should be the one to exact revenge. Not only Nabal but anyone that placed themselves in the position as my enemy. Abigail was right; I promised not to attack Nabal, and she gave us what she had figured to be a fair payment. About 10 days later, I heard that Nabal was dead; not from anything that I had done, but from God's righteous judgment. God had prevented me from making a HUGE mistake and I praised Him for that! I asked Abigail to be my wife and she accepted. She would later give birth to four sons; Amnon; Kileab; Absolam, and Adonijah. What a nightmare that would turn out to be, but I'll get to that later.

Finally, peace for my men and me. No more running, or so it seemed. Several months later, the Ziphites stirred the pot again. They reminded Saul of his hatred for me and told him of our whereabouts. Saul brought 3000 of his best men to kill me. One night while everyone in Saul's camp was asleep; Abishai and I snuck into Saul's tent. I should have left Abishai back at our camp, because he wanted to kill Saul, and I had to talk him out of it. I reminded him that Saul was the king that God gave to Israel and that opposing Saul was the same as opposing God. He agreed, and we took Saul's spear and a jug of water that was beside his head and left his camp. At daybreak, I went

to the top of the hillside and called out to Abner. "Aren't
you the man, and aren't you responsible for protecting the
king? You should be put to death; for you have failed in
your duties. I could have killed Saul while you slept." As
I spoke, Saul recognized my voice and called out to me.
When I explained that I had been in his tent and could
have killed him, he was shocked (to say the least). I showed
him his spear as proof and he was ashamed because I was
merciful unto him a second time and spared his life. Then
Saul said, "Blessed are you, my son David; you will both
accomplish much and surely prevail." He then went home
and we set out for Gath.

"God, there is something really wrong with this picture.
Living amongst the Philistines feels more like home, than
living in my own land. Achish, Israel's greatest enemy;
treats me and my men better than Saul; to whom I have
sworn allegiance to, and never betrayed his trust. I have to
believe this is all a part of Your plan even though I don't
understand it." Living in Gath is very strange; I spoke
with Achish and he gave us Ziklag to dwell in. We dwelt in
Philistia for 16 months. While in Ziklag, we fought against
the Geshurites, the Gezrites, and the Amalekites. We left
no one alive so they could not tell the king what we had
done. When we returned with our spoils to present to
Achish, he would inquire where we had been. I would tell
him, south of Judah, south of Jerahmeel and south of Ken.
Yes, he was left with the impression that we were attacking
the Israelites, but don't blame me. I truthfully answered
his question of where I had been. He never inquired as to
whom we had fought. Achish was so confident that I was
completely loyal to him that he ordered me and my men to
join his army as they prepared for battle against Saul. He
even made me his bodyguard. We made camp in Shunem
while Saul gathered Israel in Gilboa. "Okay God, how is
this going to work out. I am loyal to King Achish because

he has provided our families with a place to live in peace. However, you know I have ultimate loyalty to You and will not fight against Saul nor my people." The following morning, we marched to Aphek and the Israelites to Jezreel. While in Aphek the generals inspected the army, and notice we are with them. They stated their displeasure and mistrust to the king. Despite my apparent objections, the king sent me and my men back to Ziklag. So once again God has worked out a potentially sticky situation. I have remained loyal to both Achish and Saul, and have not had to fight against my countrymen. What a mighty God!!

Upon returning to Ziklag, we found it burned and our possessions and families taken. Understandably, my men were upset with me for leaving their families defenseless. I inquired of the Lord if we should pursue those that destroyed our homes, and God said: "pursue and recover all." We gave chase and reached the brook of Besor. 200 of the men were too tired to continue; so we left them there and continued on. My scouts found an Egyptian left in a field to die. We fed him and inquire about what he was doing there. He revealed that he was part of the Amalekite raiding party that attacked Ziklag. He agreed to take us to their hiding place as long as I agreed not to kill him or turn him over to his master. He leads us to their camp, and we slaughtered all but 400 young men that got away on camels. As God had promised; we recovered everything taken from us. We also took everything the Amalekites had taken from other places. We returned to Besor to join the 200 men that we had left behind. While there; an argument broke out regarding the spoils. Some of the men thought it was unfair that the 200 men that did not fight; should get a share of the spoils. I said that since God delivered the Amalekites into our hands, and had lost nothing taken, nor was there a loss of life, every man should get an equal share. God had shown great generosity toward them; so they should do likewise. This shall be the statute and ordinance in Israel forever.

On the third day after recovering our families from the Amalekites; a stranger came to deliver news of Saul's death. When I asked how he came about this news; he explained that he had come across the aftermath of a battle. He found Saul on the ground; badly wounded. He continued on to say, "Saul asked me to kill him so that the Philistines could not, and I did so." We all lamented Saul's death and fasted until sundown. After we mourned for Saul, Jonathan, and Israel's fallen, I asked the stranger who he was, and he stated that he was an Amalekite. Then I said, "How was it that you were not afraid to kill the Lord's anointed?" Then I called one of my men over and ordered him to kill the Amalekite. Then I ordered the sons of Judah, should be taught the Song of Bow. How art the mighty fallen... (1 Samuel 1:19-27)

The Lord had told me to go to Hebron. Upon arriving there I was anointed king over Judah. I was made aware that men from Jabesh-gilead were responsible for recovering Saul's body and burying him. I sent messengers to them, to show my gratitude. After nearly two years of fighting for control of Israel and after the tragic death of Abner, the two kingdoms were united under my rule. It's been seven and a half years here in Hebron; the kingdom is united; I got Michal back, and God is greatly to be praised! I think it's time we moved to Jerusalem.

Wouldn't you know it; just when it looked like everything was going smoothly; here come the Philistines. God told me to go out against them, and He would deliver them into my hand. We fought them at Baal-perazim, and it was said: "the Lord has broken upon my enemies like the breach of waters." The Philistines are apparently slow of learning; they made ready to attack again at Rephaim. I asked the Lord for instructions, and He responded, "Do not go straight at them. Circle behind them and attack them in front of the balsam trees. As soon as you hear the sound of marching in the tops of the trees; move in quickly. I did as the Lord commanded and smote them from Gibeon to Gezer.

You know, I'm feeling like it's time to bring the ark of God home to Jerusalem. So, I got 30,000 of my best men and head out for Gibeah. We got the ark from Abinadab's house and placed it on a new cart. Abinadab's sons, Uzza and Ahio drove the cart. On our journey back to Jerusalem, we praised God with all manner of instruments. As we approached the threshing floor of Nachon the oxen stumbled, and the cart began to shake. Uzza grabbed the ark to steady it, and God killed him instantly. I was upset that God would do such a thing, and I called the name of that place Perez-uzzah (the breach of Uzzah). Instead of continuing to Jerusalem, we took the ark to Obed-edom's house, and it stayed there for three months. Honestly, I should have known better than to put the ark of God on a cart. It has always been carried on the shoulders of the priests; this time should have been no different. Obed's house and everything about it were blessed while the ark was there. After returning to Obed's house to recover the ark of God; we carried it on the shoulders of the priest. After the first six steps; I sacrificed an ox and the fatlings and I danced before the Lord with all my might. We shouted and played instruments all the way back to Jerusalem. We placed the ark of the Lord in the tabernacle, and I offered burnt offerings and peace offerings to the Lord. After completing the offerings; I blessed all the people in the name of the Lord. Everyone also received a cake of bread; a good piece of meat, and a flagon of wine.

Then everyone departed to their own homes. I went home to bless it, and there was Michal mad because she had seen me dancing before the ark. She felt as though I had embarrassed myself; dancing out of my clothes; down to my linen ephod; in the street before the ark. After we argued I never touched Michal again.

"Ah! Finally, peace in Israel! What a mighty God I serve! You know, it's not right that I should live in this fine house, and God's ark should dwell in a tent. Let me ask Nathan, what he thinks about me building a house for the ark to sit in." Nathan thought it was a great idea. However, later that night he came to me and said, "Thus says the Lord. Are you the one that is supposed to build Me a house to dwell in? Of all the leaders of Israel since leaving Egypt; did I ask any of them to build me a house to dwell in? I called you from the fields to lead these great people. I have been with you wherever you have gone. I have cut off your enemies from you. I will make your name greater than all the great men on the Earth. I will also make a permanent place for My people to dwell and not be disturbed again. Nor will the wicked afflict them as they have in times past. The LORD also declares to you that He will raise up your descendant after you, and will establish his kingdom. He shall build a house for My name. I will establish the throne of his kingdom forever. I will be a father to him, and when he commits iniquity; I will correct him. My lovingkindness shall not depart from him; as I took it away from Saul." After Nathan had spoken, I humbled myself before God, and said: "You are great, O Lord God; there is none like You, and there is no God besides You!"

My covenant will I not break; nor alter the thing that is gone out of my lips. (Psalms 89:34) A promise God made to me, and I should do no less. I need to find out if any descendants of Saul are still alive; so I can show kindness to them for Jonathan's sake? I found out that Jonathan's son Mephiboseth is still alive, and I will fulfill my oath to Jonathan (2 Samuel 9:2-13).

Wars and rumors of war; I'm growing tired of war. They are so bloody and can be very chaotic. We smote the Philistines and took Methegammah out of their hands. We smote Moab, and the Moabites became my servants and brought gifts. We smote also Hadadezer, the son of Rehob, king of Zobah. We took from him a thousand chariots, and seven hundred horsemen, and twenty thousand footmen. We slew twenty-two thousand men of the Syrians. Then I put garrisons in Syria, and the Syrians became my servants and brought gifts. The LORD preserved me wherever I went. I took the shields of gold that were on the servants of Hadadezer and brought them to Jerusalem. When Toi king of Hamath heard that I had smitten all the host of Hadadezer. He sent Joram his son unto me; to salute and to bless me, because I had fought against Hadadezer, and had smitten him. Joram brought with him vessels of silver, gold, of brass. I dedicated unto the LORD all the silver and gold that I had received of all nations which I had subdued. I got a name when I returned from smiting of the Syrians in the valley of salt; being eighteen thousand men. I put garrisons in Edom, and they became my servants.

At what point do they understand; God is with me and the army of God cannot be defeated? In the spring, I sent Joab and the army out to fight the Ammonite while I stayed at home. When night fell, I went out onto the roof and saw the most beautiful woman in all of Israel. I inquired as to who she was and sent for her. I slept with her despite her being married to Uriah the Hittite (one of my best soldiers). Wouldn't you know it; I got her pregnant and now I've got to cover up my mess. I sent word to Joab to send Uriah home. When he arrived; I asked how the battle was going and told him to go home. I sent some meat to his house. Later I found out that he slept at my doorstep. I called Uriah asked him why he didn't go home. He replied that the ark of God was in a tent; Joab and his men were in an open field, and I would not go to my house and eat and lay with my wife while they could not. Now that is what you call loyalty to your brothers in arms, and it kind of made sense, but he is messing up my plan! Then I told Uriah to stay in Jerusalem until tomorrow and he can return to battle. Later that day I brought him to my house, fed him and got him drunk. Then I sent him home to his wife. Again, he did not go home; so I sent him back to the battle with a letter to Joab. A few days later I received word that Uriah had been killed in battle (just like I planned). After Bathsheba had mourned the death of her husband; I married her and now I'm in the clear. Or so I thought.

Nathan stopped by one day, and he told me a story. "There were two men in one city; one rich, and the other poor. The rich man had exceeding many flocks and herds, but the poor man had nothing, except one little ewe lamb. He had bought and nourished it, and it grew up together with him, and with his children. It did eat of his own meat and drank of his own cup. It laid in his bosom and was like a daughter unto him. There came a traveler unto the rich man, and he did not take of his own flock and of his own herd, to dress for the wayfaring man that was come unto him. He took the poor man's lamb, and dressed it for the man that had come to him." My anger was greatly kindled against the man; and I said to Nathan, "As the LORD lives, the man that has done this thing shall surely die! He shall restore the lamb fourfold, because he did this thing, and because he had no pity." Then Nathan said, "Thou art the man! Thus, saith the LORD God of Israel; I anointed thee

king over Israel, and I delivered thee out of the hand of
Saul. I gave you your master's house, and your master's
wives into your bosom. I gave you the house of Israel and
Judah, and if that had been too little; I would moreover
have given unto you such and such things. Why have you
despised the commandment of the LORD; to do evil in His
sight? You have killed Uriah the Hittite with the sword,
and have taken his wife to be your wife. Now; therefore,
the sword will never depart from your house, because you
have despised Me, and have taken the wife of Uriah the
Hittite to be your wife. Behold, I will raise up evil against
you out of your own house. I will take your wives before
your eyes, and give them unto your neighbor. He shall
lie with your wives in the sight of this sun because you
did this secretly. I will do this thing before all Israel, and
before the sun." I said unto Nathan, "I have sinned against
the LORD." Then Nathan said unto me, "The LORD also has
put away your sin; you shall not die. Howbeit, because by
this deed you have given great occasion to the enemies of
the LORD to blaspheme. The child that is born unto you
shall surely die." Nathan departed unto his house, and
the LORD struck the child that Bathsheba bare unto me,
and it was very sick. I sought God for the child and fasted.
I went in, and laid all night upon the earth... "Against You,
and You only have I sinned, and done this evil in Your
sight. That You might be justified when You speak and be
clear when You judge. Purge me with hyssop, and I will be
clean. Wash me, and I will be whiter than snow. Create in
me a clean heart, O God; renew a right spirit within me.
Cast me not away from thy presence, and take not your
holy spirit from me. Deliver me from bloodguiltiness, O
God of my salvation, and my tongue shall sing aloud of
thy righteousness..." (Psalms 51) The elders of his house
arose and tried to raise me up from the earth, but I would
not. Neither did I eat bread with them. On the seventh
day; the child died. Then I got up from the ground and

washed. I anointed myself and changed my clothes. I went into the house of the LORD and worshipped. Then I comforted Bathsheba, and went in unto her, and lay with her. She bore a son, and I called his name Solomon, and the LORD loved him.

It certainly didn't take long for God's judgment to fall. My baby is dead, and now I heard Amnon has lusted after his sister Tamar. He allowed Jonadab to convince him it's okay to lay with her because he is the son of a king. Amnon raped Tamar and added to her shame by sending her away in anger. After he violated her; he despised her more than he had loved her. Tamar told Absalom what Amnon did, and Absalom had Amnon killed. Absalom fled to Geshur for three years in fear for his life. Joab put together a pretty good scheme; to convince me to allow Absalom to come back home (2 Samuel 14:1-23). I agreed that he could return to Jerusalem, but I didn't want to see his face. After two years, Absalom's frustration got the best of him again, and he set Joab's field on fire because Joab ignored his summons. Joab told me that Absalom wants to see me, and I agreed. Absalom came in and humbled himself before me, and we reconciled our differences. Or so I thought. Come to find out; Absalom had come up with a plot to take my throne. He had gone to Hebron and on the advice of Ahithophel; proclaimed himself king of Israel. Since all the men of Israel are with Absalom; my servants and I fled to the Mount of Olives where we were met by Hushai the Archite. I said to him "If you pass over with me; then you will be a burden to me. If you return to the city and say to Absalom, 'I will be your servant, O king; as I have been your father's servant in time past. Then you can thwart the counsel of Ahithophel for me. (Hushai's counsel to Absalom: 2 Samuel 18). We made it to Mahanaim and were fed by Shobi and rested. The next day Joab and 600 men went to the forest of Ephraim to fight Absalom and Israel.

The people of Israel were defeated there, and the slaughter that day was great, 20,000 men. When I was told about the battle; I asked about Absalom and was told he was dead. I went to the rooftop and wept saying "O my son Absalom, my son, my son Absalom! Would I had died instead of you; O Absalom, my son, my son!" Later I returned to Jerusalem as king, but not without contention. Sheba, the son of Bichri, a Benjamite, blew the trumpet and said, "We have no portion in David; nor do we have an inheritance in the son of Jesse. Every man to his tents, O Israel!" So all the men of Israel followed Sheba. I perceived that Sheba would cause more trouble than Absalom. So I sent Abashai and Joab after him. They followed him to Abel Beth-maacah, and they cast up a siege ramp against the city. All the people who were with Joab were wreaking destruction to topple the wall. The people of Abel; being peaceful people cut off Sheba's head, and threw it over the wall to Joab, to save the city. So, Joab and his men returned to Jerusalem.

As if there hasn't been enough going on; a famine hit Israel and continued for three years. I sought the presence of the LORD, and the LORD said, "It is for Saul and his bloody house because he put the Gibeonites to death." The sons of Israel had made a covenant with them, but Saul had sought to kill them in his zeal for the sons of Israel and Judah. Then I said to the Gibeonites, "What should I do for you? How can I make atonement; that you may bless the inheritance of the LORD?" They replied, "The man who consumed us, and who planned to exterminate us from remaining within any border of Israel; let seven men from his sons be given to us. We will hang them before the LORD in Gibeah of Saul; the chosen of the LORD." "I will give them," I said. However, I spared Mephibosheth, the son of Jonathan, because of the oath of the LORD which was between us. Meanwhile, I ordered the bones of Saul and Jonathan should be taken from Jabesh-gilead and buried in Zela of Benjamin. After that, God was moved by prayer for the land, and the famine ended.

Once again, the anger of the LORD was kindled against Israel, and I ordered Joab to number Israel and Judah. So, Joab and the captains of the host went to number the people of Israel. They passed over Jordan and pitched in Aroer; on the right side of the city that lieth amid the river of Gad, and toward Jazer. Then they came to Gilead; Tahtimhodshi; Danjaan, and about to Zidon. Then to the stronghold of Tyre; to all the cities of the Hivites; and of the Canaanites; then south of Judah, and to Beersheba. So, when they had gone through all the land; they came to Jerusalem at the end of nine months and twenty days. Then Joab gave up the sum of the number of the people to me, and there were in Israel eight hundred thousand valiant men that drew the sword. The men of Judah were five hundred thousand men. I was ashamed after that, and I said unto the LORD, "I have sinned greatly in what I have done. Now, I beseech you, O LORD, take away the iniquity of thy servant; for I have done very foolishly." In the morning, the word of the LORD came to the prophet Gad saying, "Go and say unto David, thus saith the LORD, I offer you three things. Choose one of them, that I may do it unto you." So, Gad came to me, and told me, and said unto me, "Shall seven years of famine come unto thee in thy land? Will you flee three months before your enemies; while they pursue you? Or that there be three days› pestilence in the land? I said unto Gad, "I am between a rock and a hard place. Let us fall now into the hand of the LORD; for his mercies are great. Let me not fall into the hand of man." So, the LORD sent a pestilence upon Israel from the morning; even to the time appointed. During that time; there died of the people from Dan even to Beersheba seventy thousand men. When the angel stretched out his hand upon Jerusalem to destroy it; the LORD repented of the evil. He said to the angel that destroyed the people, "It is enough. Stay now your hand", and the angel of the LORD was by the threshing place of Araunah the Jebusite. I spoke unto the LORD when I saw the angel that smote the people, and I said, "Lo, I have sinned, and I have done wickedly, but these sheep, what have they done? Let your hand; I pray thee; be against me, and my father's house." Then Gad came to me, and said, "Go up, rear an altar unto the LORD in the threshing floor of Araunah the Jebusite, and I went up as the LORD commanded. Araunah looked and saw me and my servants coming toward him, and Araunah came and bowed himself on his face upon the ground. Then he said, unto me, "Wherefore is my lord the king come to his servant?" I replied, "to buy the threshing floor of thee; so that I may build an altar unto the LORD; that the plague may be stayed from the people." Araunah said "Let my lord the king take and offer up what seems good unto you. Here are oxen for burnt sacrifice, and threshing instruments and other instruments of the oxen for wood. I replied unto Araunah, "Not so; but I will surely buy it from you at a price: I will not offer burnt offerings unto the LORD my God; of that which did not cost me anything." So, I bought the threshing floor and the oxen for fifty shekels of silver and built there an altar unto the LORD. I offered burnt offerings and peace offerings. So, the LORD was intreated for the land, and the plague stayed from Israel.

My time upon this Earth is growing short, and I have had a long journey from lowly shepherd to the king; from a liar to honest before God; from musician to a murderer, and from fearful to a mighty man. I've spent 40 years ruling over all of Israel. God has established my throne forever! There were times that I was a huge disappointment in my dealings and other times that I was an example for all to follow. Although, I made some very horrible mistakes; I never made excuses or blamed someone else for them. I never lost sight of God, and what he expected of me. I always knew the importance of humbling myself before God, and to accept the consequences for my actions. I also knew that praise and worship are an essential part of living for God, and He alone is worthy of all my praise. Now as my last act as king: Israel and Judah will know that my throne will be passed to Solomon; not to Adonijah who has sought to take Israel for his own (1 Kings 1:5-37).

Now my final word to Solomon; "Be strong and show yourself a man. Keep the charge of the LORD thy God; walk in His ways. Keep His statutes and His commandments. Keep His judgments, and His testimonies; as it is written in the law of Moses. Moreover, you know also what Joab the son of Zeruiah did to me, and what he did to the two captains of the hosts of Israel. What he did unto Abner the son of Ner, and unto Amasa the son of Jether. How he slew them and shed the blood of war in peace. He put the blood of war upon his girdle that was about his loins, and in his shoes, that were on his feet. Do therefore according to your wisdom, and do not let him go down to the grave in peace. Show kindness unto the sons of Barzillai the Gileadite, and let them eat at your table because they came to me when I fled from Absalom your brother. Behold, you have with you Shimei the son of Gera, a Benjamite of Bahurim, which cursed me with a grievous curse in the day when I went to Mahanaim, but he came down to meet me at Jordan, and I swore to him by the LORD, saying, I will not put you to death with the sword. Now; therefore, do not hold him guiltless: for you are a wise man, and know what you ought to do unto him.

Elijah: First Look at Manic-Depression

Have you ever experienced periods of alternating highs and lows? How about serious mood swings? Well, welcome to my world! Oh, and I'll bet, you like how I just popped up out of nowhere too: didn't you? Since the scripture didn't bother to mention my early years, I won't bother to bore you with the details. God called me to warn that reprobate of a king, Ahab, of the impending doom headed toward Israel. With more than 80 years of poor leadership since David was king, Ahab's reign got off to a pretty bad start. In fact, it is said that he did evil in the sight of the LORD more than all who were before him. Then it was as though it had been a trivial thing for him to walk in the sins of Jeroboam when he married Jezebel, and went to serve Baal and worshiped him. Then things went from bad to worse. She added a whole new dimension to the idolatry that had gripped Israel. Ahab erected an altar for Baal in the house of Baal which he built in Samaria and also made the Asherah (Phoenician goddess). Therefore, Ahab did more to provoke the LORD God of Israel than all the kings of Israel who were before him.

At the appointed time, I met Ahab and said: "As the LORD, the God of Israel lives; there shall be neither dew nor rain; unless I say so." Then God spoke to me and said, "Go and hide by the brook called Cherith; which is east of the Jordan. You will drink of the brook, and I have commanded the ravens to provide for you there." Strange that God would choose an unclean bird to provide for me, but who am I to question Him. As you would expect, the brook dried up and God spoke to me and said, "Arise, go to Zarephath; which belongs to Sidon and stay there. I have commanded a widow there to provide for you."

I did as God commanded, and when I met the widow,

I asked her for a cup of water. As she was going to get the water, I called out to her and asked for a piece of bread also. She replied, "I have no bread, I only have a handful of flour and a little bit of oil." She was expecting to prepare a cake for herself and her son to eat and then die. I'm thinking, this isn't making any sense. First You use an unclean bird, and now a woman that can't take care of herself or her son. How is this going to work out? Then I said to the woman "Do not fear, make me a little bread cake and bring it out to me, after that; make one for yourself and your son. The LORD God of Israel has assured me; the jar of flour shall not be exhausted, nor shall the jug of oil be empty until the day that the LORD sends rain on the face of the Earth." So, she did what I asked, and we had food to eat every day.

As time passed, the widow's son got sick. His illness grew worse and he died. "O man of God," said the woman, "what have you done to me? Have you come to remind me of my iniquity and cause the death of my son?" Here goes my brain again, but now it's in overdrive. Can I get a break? God, this woman's son has died and she is blaming me. Why is this happening? She has been more than generous under the circumstances. What am I to do? I took the boy from her and carried him to my room and laid him on the bed. I prayed. "O LORD my God, have You also brought tragedy to this widow, by causing her son to die?" I laid on top of the child and continued to pray; "O LORD my God, I pray You, let this child's life return to him." The Lord heard my prayer and answered. The child revived, and I took him down to his mother. She said, "Now I know that you are a man of God and that the word of the LORD from your mouth is truth." Another miracle from God. Surely, He has proven himself worthy of honor and glory.

Three years have passed and no rain, but God has sustained us. Then God spoke to me and said, "Go to Ahab and I will send rain upon the Earth." On my way to meet Ahab, I saw Obadiah and told him to let Ahab know I was coming to see him. He strongly objected for fear of his life (1 Kings 18:8-14). I reassured him that I would meet Ahab today and he did as I commanded. Ahab saw me from a distance and came out to meet me. When he reached me, and said, "Is this you, the trouble maker of Israel?" I replied "I have not troubled Israel, but you and your father's house have because you have forsaken the commandments of the LORD and you have followed the Baals. Now, gather to me all of Israel; together with 450 prophets of Baal, and 400 prophets of Asherah, (who eat at Jezebel's table) at Mount Carmel." Ahab sent word to the prophets and had all of Israel to come to Mount Carmel. When everyone had arrived, I questioned the people, "How long will you waver between two opinions? If the LORD is God; follow Him. If Baal is; follow him." While everyone looked at me like I had lost my mind, I continued. "I alone am left as a prophet of the LORD, but Baal's prophets are 450 men. Now give us two oxen, and let them choose one ox for themselves and cut it up. Then place it on the wood, but don't put a fire under it. I will prepare the other ox and lay it on the wood. I will not put a fire under it. Then you call on the name of your god, and I will call on the name of the LORD. The God who answers by fire, He is God." All the people agreed; that was a good idea.

So, the prophets of Baal took their ox, prepared it, and placed it on the altar they had built. They called out to Baal saying, "O Baal, answer us." They did this for six hours, and there was no answer. Then they began to leap around the altar and I called out to them saying, "Call out with a loud voice, for he is a god; either he is occupied or gone aside. Perhaps he is on a journey, or maybe he is asleep and needs to be awakened." The prophets cried louder, and began to cut themselves according to their custom until the evening sacrifice, and still no answer. Then I called all the people to gather around, and I repaired the altar of the Lord which had been torn down. After that, I dug a trench around the altar. Then I prepared the ox and placed it on the altar, and commanded the people to get four pitchers of water and to pour it on the ox and the wood. They did that three times, so that water flowed around the altar. Yeah, I know! You're probably wondering where the water came from. After a three-year drought; there shouldn't be any; right? There are some questions that don't need answering; therefore, I don't ask. After all, if God can produce flour and oil, why wouldn't He be able to produce water? Then I had them fill the trench also. At the time of the evening sacrifice, I called, "O LORD, the God of Abraham, Isaac, and Israel, today let it be known that You are God in Israel and that I am Your servant. Also, I have done all these things at Your word. Answer me O LORD; answer me that these people may know that You; O LORD; are God and that You have turned their heart back again." Then the fire of the Lord fell and consumed the offering, the wood, and the stones. It also dried up the water that was in the trench. When all the people saw it; they fell on their faces. They said, "The LORD, He is God; the LORD, He is God." Then I commanded the people to seize the prophets of Baal; do not let one of them escape. They seized them, and I took them down to the brook Kishon, and slew them there.

After that, I told Ahab, "Go, eat and drink because I hear the sound of an abundance of rain." Ahab left and I went back to the top of Mount Carmel. I sat down and put my head between my knees. I told my servant to go look toward the sea. He did so and returned saying, "I saw nothing." I sent him seven times, and on the seventh time he returned and said, "There, is a cloud as small as a man's hand coming up from the sea." So, I said, "Go up, say to Ahab, prepare your chariot and go down, so that the rain does not stop you." After a while the sky got dark and the rain fell. The hand of the Lord came upon me and I outran Ahab's chariot back to Jezreel.

After Ahab told Jezebel what happened, she was VERY

livid. She sent a message to me saying, "May the gods do to me and even more if I do not make your life as the life of one of them by this time tomorrow." I got scared and ran to Beersheba; then went a day's journey into the wilderness and sat under a Juniper tree. Then I said, "I've had enough; now, O LORD, take my life, for I am not better than my fathers." Now I just killed 450 men, so why am I afraid of a threat from this woman? I fell asleep under the Juniper tree and was awaken by an angel. He gave me food and water. After I ate, I went back to sleep. The angel woke me up a second time and I ate again. After I ate; I went to Horeb. I found a cave to rest in, and the voice of the Lord came to me and said. "What are you doing here?" I replied, "I have done all that you've asked of me because the sons of Israel have forsaken Your covenant; torn down Your altars and killed Your prophets with the sword. Now I alone am left, and they want to kill me." God replied "Go out and stand on the mountain before the LORD. Behold, I am about to pass by." A great and mighty wind tore into the mountains and shattered the rocks before the LORD, but the LORD was not in the wind. After the wind, there was an earthquake, but the LORD was not in the earthquake. After the earthquake, a fire, but the LORD was not in the fire, and after the fire a sound of a still small voice. When I heard it; I wrapped my face in my mantle and went out and stood in the entrance of the cave. Then a voice came to me and said, "What are you doing here? Go, return to the wilderness of Damascus, and when you have arrived, anoint Hazael (khaz-aw-ale') king over Aram. Anoint Jehu the son of Nimshi (nim-shee') king over Israel, and Elisha the son of Shaphat (shaw-fawt') of Abel-meholah (aw-bale' mekh-o-law') as a prophet in your place. It shall come about, the one who escapes from the sword of Hazael; Jehu shall put to death. The one who escapes from the sword of Jehu; Elisha shall put to death. Yet I will leave 7,000 in Israel that have not bowed to Baal and every mouth that has not kissed him."

So, I departed from Horeb and found Elisha the son of Shaphat, while he was plowing with twelve pairs of oxen. I passed by him and threw my mantle on him. He left the oxen and ran after me and said, "Please let me kiss my father and my mother; then I will follow you." I replied, "Go back again, for what have I done to you?" He returned from following me, and took a pair of oxen and sacrificed them, and boiled their flesh, and gave it to the people and they ate. Then he got up and followed me and ministered to me.

Here's something for you to ponder. Why do people that have the most, covet the thing(s) of people that have the least? How can people be that greedy? Ahab king of Israel isn't satisfied with the land that he has; he wants Naboth vineyard because it's close to the palace. I'll give him a slight break though because he did offer to trade or to purchase it. However, when Naboth refused both options; he went back to the palace and pouted. When Jezebel saw him pouting; she inquires as to why? He responded, "Because I spoke to Naboth the Jezreelite and said to him, 'Give me your vineyard for money; or else, if it pleases you, I will give you a vineyard in its place, but he said, "I will not give you my vineyard." Jezebel said to him, "Do you now reign over Israel? Arise, eat bread, and let your heart be joyful; I will give you the vineyard of Naboth." So, Jezebel wrote a letter to the city elders and they killed Naboth. (1Kings 21:7-14) As Ahab was on his way to take possession of Naboth vineyard I met him and said, "Thus says the LORD, have you murdered and also taken possession? In the place where the dogs licked up the blood of Naboth; the dogs will lick up your blood." Ahab said, "You have found me out, O my enemy?" I answered, "I have found you out because you have sold yourself to do evil in the sight of the LORD." Then the Lord said, "Behold, I will bring evil upon you, and I will sweep you away and will cut off every male from you. Both bond and free in Israel, and I will make your house like the house of Jeroboam, and like the house of Baasha (bah-shaw'), because of the aggravation by which you have provoked Me to anger, and because you have made Israel sin. As for Jezebel; the dogs will eat her in the district of Jezreel. Surely there was no one like Ahab who sold himself to do evil in the sight of the LORD because Jezebel his wife incited him. He acted atrociously in following idols, according to all that the Amorites had done; whom the LORD cast out before the sons of Israel." It came about when Ahab heard these words, that he tore his clothes and put on sackcloth and fasted, and he lay in sackcloth and went about dejectedly. Then the Lord said to me, "Do you see how Ahab has humbled himself before Me? Because he has humbled himself before Me; I will not bring the evil in his days, but I will bring the evil upon his house in his son's days."

Three years later, Ahab died according to the prophecy of Micaiah (me-kaw-yeh-hoo') and his son Ahaziah (akh-az-yaw') became king in his place. He reigned two years over Israel. He also did evil in the sight of the LORD, and walked in the way of his father, and in the way of his mother and in the way of Jeroboam who caused Israel to sin. He served and worshiped Baal and provoked the LORD God of Israel to anger. Ahaziah became ill and he sent messengers and said to them, "Go, inquire of Baal-zebub, the god of Ekron, whether I will recover from this sickness." The angel of the LORD said to me, "Arise, go up to meet the messengers of Ahaziah and say to them, 'Is it because there is no God in Israel that you are going to inquire of Baal-zebub, the god of Ekron? Now, therefore, thus says the LORD, you shall not get up from the bed that you are on, but you shall surely die." Then I went on my way.

Here I am sitting on a hillside; minding my own business; enjoying the day and a captain with fifty men, came up the hillside and said, "O man of God, the king said to come down." Seriously? Who does he think he is? Am I a little kid that he thinks he can order around? I replied, "if I am a man of God, let fire come down and consume you and your fifty." No sooner than I finished speaking; fire fell from heaven and consumed the fifty-one men. Later, another captain, with his fifty men came up the hillside and said, "man of God, the king said come quickly." Ok, this reprobate really doesn't know who's he's dealing with. I replied again, "if I am a man of God; let fire come down and consume you and your fifty." Just as before, fire falls from heaven and consumes the captain with his fifty men. Maybe that will convince Ahaziah, he's in no position to issue orders. Or maybe not. Here comes the third group of fifty-one. However, this captain came with a different approach. If no one else gets it; at least this captain got it. He came and bowed down on his knees and begged and said, "O man of God, please let my life and the lives of these fifty servants of yours be precious in your sight. Behold fire came down from heaven and consumed the first two captains of fifty with their fifties, but now let my life be precious in your sight." Then the angel of the LORD said to me, "Go down with him; do not be afraid of him." So, I arose and went down with him to the king. When I got to the king I said, "Thus says the LORD, 'Is there no God in Israel for you to inquire of His word? Is that why you have sent messengers to inquire of Baal-zebub, the god of Ekron?' Therefore, you shall not recover from your injury, but shall surely die." So Ahaziah died according to the word of the LORD which I had spoken. Because he had no son, Jehoram the son of Jehoshaphat became king in his place.

Having done all that the Lord had commanded me to do and say, the time has come for me to leave this place. The Lord told me to leave Gilgal and to go to Bethel. I said to Elisha, "Stay here please, for the LORD is sending me to Bethel." Elisha said, "As the LORD lives and as you live, I will not leave you." So, we went down to Bethel. While there; the sons of the prophets who were at Bethel came out to Elisha and said, "Do you know that the LORD will take away your master from over you today?" He said, "Yes; I know; be still." Then, I said to Elisha, "please stay here, for the LORD is sending me to Jericho." He said, "As the LORD lives, and as you live, I will not leave you." So, we went to Jericho. While at Jericho the sons of the prophets approached Elisha and said, "Do you know the Lord will take your master from you today?" He answered, "Yes; I know. Be still!" I turned to Elisha and said, "Please stay here; the Lord is sending me to the Jordan River." He replied, As the Lord lives and as you live; I will not leave your side." So, we continued on our journey. When we arrived at the Jordan; I took off my mantle, and folded it together. I struck the water, and it divided. Then we crossed over on dry ground.

After crossing over the Jordan; I said to Elisha, "Tell me; what can I do for you before I am taken away from you." He responded, "Please let me have a double portion of your spirit." Not expecting that response; I said, "You have asked a hard thing; nevertheless, if you see me when I am taken from you; it shall be so. If you do not see me; it will not be so." As we are walking along and talking; a chariot and horses of fires appeared, and separated us. I stepped onto the chariot, and it parted by a whirlwind to heaven. As I was going up; my mantle flew off of my shoulders and fell to the ground.

Elisha: Twice the Adventure

Be careful what you ask for; because you just might get it! I asked for a double portion of Elijah's spirit, and I'm thinking I should have been a little more specific. I mean people dying because of what you let come out of your mouth can mess with your head; if you know what I mean. We'll deal with that later. For a minute; it didn't look like I was going to get exactly double either. Who knew, it would be after my death that I would get exactly double. Amazing, absolutely amazing! Ready for the adventure of a lifetime? Let's get to it.

My master (teacher), friend, Elijah; what a character. A man with some of the highest highs you could ever witness, and unfortunately, some of the most depressing lows. I was in awe when I saw him taken up into heaven in a whirlwind. I saw it and cried out, "My father, my father, the chariots of Israel and its horsemen!" Then I took hold of my clothes and tore them into two pieces. You would think that it would be a very exciting event (and it was!), but there was also a profound sense of loss. I guess that's why I tore my clothes. I'm not sure, but as I was doing it, Elijah's mantle was falling from the sky. I picked up the mantle and returned to the bank of the Jordan River. I struck the water with the mantel and said, "Where is the LORD, the God of Elijah?" As soon as the mantel hit the water, the water divided and I crossed over on dry ground. Wow, what a feeling! Now I know without a doubt that God is with me. It has begun! When the sons of the prophets who were at Jericho saw this, they said, "The spirit of Elijah rests on Elisha", and they came to meet me and bowed themselves to the ground before me. They said, "Behold now, there are fifty strong men with your servants; please let them go and search for your master. Perhaps the Spirit of the LORD has taken him up, and cast him on some mountain or into some valley." I replied, "There is no need", but they pushed and pushed. They continued to press the issue until I gave in. I consented to the search, and the fifty men went out. After three days of searching; they found nothing, and I said to them, "Didn't I tell you, do not go?"

While I was in Jericho, the men of the city said to me, "Everything in this city is pleasant; as my lord sees. However, the water is bad and the land is barren." I asked for a new jar with salt in it. They brought it to me. I went out to the spring, and threw the salt in, saying, "Thus says the LORD; I have purified these waters, death and barrenness shall not come out of it any longer." Now the waters were purified; according to the word which I had spoken. After that, I left for Bethel. As I was about to enter Bethel; young boys came out of the city. They mocked me saying, "Go up you baldhead; go up you baldhead!" Not sure why them calling me baldhead bothered me so much, but it did. I mean, after all, I am bald. Without hesitation; I looked back at them. Then I cursed them in the name of the LORD. Shortly thereafter, two female bears came out of the woods and tore them apart; forty-two boys in all. I'll bet you nobody else will call me baldhead! From Bethel, I continued to Mount Carmel, and then to Samaria.

Now Jehoram son of Ahab became king of Israel, and he reigned in Samaria twelve years. He did evil in the sight of the LORD, but not like his father and his mother. He had put away the sacred pillar of Baal which his father had made. Nevertheless, he clung to the sins of Jeroboam. Now Mesha (may-shaw') king of Moab broke his treaty with Israel and King Jehoram went out of Samaria and gathered all Israel for war. (2 Kings 3: 3-12)

As the army of Israel approached me, I said to King Jehoram, "What do I have to do with you? Go to the prophets of your father and your mother." The king of Israel replied, "No, for the LORD has called these three kings together to give them into the hand of Moab." I said, "As the LORD of hosts lives; were it not that I regard the presence of Jehoshaphat the king of Judah; I would not look at you nor see you. Now bring me a minstrel". When the minstrel played; the spirit of the LORD came upon me. "Thus says the LORD; make this valley full of trenches. You will not see wind or rain, yet the valley shall be filled with water; so that you shall drink; both you and your cattle and your beasts. This is just a small thing in the sight of the LORD; He will also give the Moabites into your hand. Then you shall strike every fortified city and every choice city; tear down every good tree and stop all springs of water. Then mar every good piece of land with stones."

Everything was done according to the word of the Lord and early in the morning; the sun shone on the water, and the Moabites saw the water as red as blood. They said, "This is blood; the kings have surely fought each other, and they have slain one another. Now therefore, Moab to the spoil!" However, when they came to the camp of Israel; the Israelites arose and struck them. They went into the land; slaughtering the Moabites. They destroyed the cities, and each one threw a stone on every piece of good land and filled it. They stopped all the springs of water and cut down all the good trees. When the king of Moab saw that the battle was too ferocious for him; he took 700 men who drew swords to break through the Israelite's line, but they could not.

Sometime later a certain woman came to me with a request. I said, "What can I do for you? Her husband died and the creditor had come to take her two children to be his slaves. Then I inquired of her, "Tell me, what do you have in the house?" She said, "Your maidservant has nothing in the house except a jar of oil." I told her, "Go borrow vessels from all your neighbors. Not just a few; get all that you can. Go in and shut the door behind you. You and your sons, pour oil into all the vessels and set aside what is full. So, she left me and shut the door behind her and her sons. They were bringing the vessels to her and she poured. When all the vessels were full, the oil stopped. She came back to me when all the vessels were full, and I said, "Go, sell the oil and pay your debt, and you and your sons can live off the rest."

Now there came a day when I went through Shunem. I met a prominent woman, and she persuaded me to eat with her and her husband. Every time I passed by; I returned there to eat. She said to her husband, "I perceive that this is a holy man of God passing by us regularly. Let's make a room and put a bed, a table, a chair, and a lampstand in it for him. So when he comes to us; he can turn in there." One day I returned, and went into the upper chamber and rested. After a while; I said to Gehazi (gay-khah-zee') my servant, "Call this Shunammite (shoo-nam-meeth')." He had called her, and she stood before him. I said to her, "You have cared for us for a while; what can I do for you? Can I speak to the king or the captain of the army on your behalf?" She answered, "I live among my people." Then Gehazi spoke up and said, "She has no son and her husband is old." I said, "At this time next year you will embrace a son." She said, "Do not play with my emotions like that my lord. How can this happen, because you know my husband is old?" I gave her no response and she walked away.

Later, the woman conceived and bore a son at that time the next year; as I had said to her. One day I noticed her coming from a distance; I said to Gehazi "Behold, here comes the Shunammite." Please run to meet her and say to her, "Is it well with you? Is it well with your husband? Is it well with the child?" She answered, "It is well." When she came to me on the hill; she caught hold of my feet. Gehazi came near to push her away, but I said, "Let her alone; for her soul is troubled and the LORD has hidden it from me." She began speaking, "The day came that my son went out with his father to the reapers. While he was working, he said to his father, 'My head, my head.' His father said to his servant, 'Carry him to his mother.' When they had brought him to me, he sat on my lap until noon, and then he died. I laid him on your bed and shut the door behind me. Then I called my husband and said, 'Please send me one of the servants and one of the donkeys, so I may run to the man of God and return.' He replied, 'Why will you go to him today? It is neither a new moon nor the Sabbath.' I said, "it will be well." Then I saddled a donkey and said to my servant, 'Drive; do not slow down the pace for me unless I tell you.'"

I was a bit shocked because I didn't quite understand why God would keep this from me. Then she said, "Did I ask for a son from my lord? Did I not say, do not play with my emotions like that?" Then I said to Gehazi, "Gird up your loins and take my staff in your hand, and go your way. If you meet any man; do not greet him. If anyone greets you; do not answer him. Go into my room, and lay my staff on the boy's face." The woman said, "As the LORD lives and as you live; I will not leave you." So, I arose and followed her. Gehazi went on before us and laid the staff on the boy's face, but there was no response. He returned to meet us and told me, "The boy has not awakened." When I went into the house; behold the boy was dead and laid on my bed. I entered the room and shut the door behind us, and prayed to the LORD. I went up and laid on the child. I put my mouth on his mouth and my eyes on his eyes and my hands on his hands, I stretched myself on him, and the flesh of the child became warm. Then I walked in the room once back and forth and went back and stretched myself on him. All of a sudden; the boy sneezed seven times and opened his eyes. I called Gehazi and said, "Call that Shunammite." When she came in, I said, "Take your son." Then she came in and fell at my feet and bowed herself to the ground, and she took her son and went out.

After that, I returned to Gilgal and there was a famine in the land. I was with the sons of the prophets and I said to my servant, "Put on the large pot and boil stew for the sons of the prophets." So, one went out into the field to gather herbs. He found a wild vine and picked from it. His pockets were full of wild gourds, but they did not know what they were. He came in and sliced them into the pot of stew. When they poured it out for the men to eat; they cried out and said, "O man of God, there is death in the pot", and they were unable to eat it. I said, "Bring me some meal." I threw it into the pot and said, "Pour it out for the people to eat." As he poured the stew it was purified.

Later, a man came from Baal-shalishah (bah'-al shaw-lee-shaw') and brought me bread of the first fruits. Twenty loaves of barley and fresh ears of corn were in his sack. I said, "Give them to the people that they may eat." My servant said, "What? Will I set this before a hundred men (women and children)?" I responded, "give them to the people that they can eat; for thus says the LORD; they shall eat and have some leftovers." So, he set it before them, and they ate and had some leftovers. Exactly as I had told them. Now for those of you that are counting; that was miracle number nine. Not that I was counting or anything.

As time passed, Naaman came to see me. Don't blink, 'cause this is a two-for-one special. Naaman was captain of the army Aram. He was a great man with his master. He was highly respected because through him the LORD had given victory to Aram. The man was also a valiant warrior. The problem was; he was a leper. Now the Arameans had gone out on a raid; they had taken captive a little girl from Israel, and she waited on Naaman's wife. She said to her mistress, "I wish that my master was with the prophet who is in Samaria! He would cure him of his leprosy." After overhearing that; Naaman went in and told his master, saying, "It was told to my wife; by the girl who is from Israel; there is a prophet in Samaria that can heal my leprosy." Then the king of Aram said, "Go now, and I will send a letter to the king of Israel." He delivered the letter to the king of Israel, and it said, "Now as this letter comes to you; I have sent Naaman my servant to you; that you may cure him of his leprosy." When the king of Israel read the letter; he tore his clothes and said, "Am I God; to kill and to make alive? Why is this man is sending word to me to cure a man of his leprosy? Is he seeking a quarrel against me?"

When I heard that the king of Israel had torn his clothes; I sent word to him saying, "Why have you torn your clothes? Send Naaman to me, and he shall know that there is a prophet in Israel." So Naaman came with his horses and his chariots and stood at my doorway. I sent a messenger to him saying, "Go and wash in the Jordan seven times, and your flesh will be restored to you, and you will be clean." Naaman was furious! He started to walk away and said, "I thought, He would surely come out to me; call on the name of the LORD his God, wave his hand over the place, and cure my leprosy. Are not Abanah (ab-aw-naw') and Pharpar (par-par'), the rivers of Damascus; better than all the waters of Israel? Could I not wash in them and be clean?" He turned and went away in a rage.

His servants came near and spoke to him saying, "My father, had the prophet told you to do some great thing; would you not have done it? How much more than; when he says to you; wash and be clean?" Naaman went down and dipped himself seven times in the Jordan, and his flesh was restored like that of a little child and he was clean. When he returned with all his company, and came and stood before me, he said, "Now I know that there is no God in all the Earth; except in Israel. Please take a gift from your servant now." I said, "As the LORD lives, I will not take anything." He urged me to take it, but I refused. Naaman asked for two loads of dirt and said "Your servant will no longer offer burnt offering nor sacrifice to other gods but unto the LORD. In this matter may the

LORD pardon me; when my master goes into the house of
Rimmon to worship there; or when he leans on my hand
and I bow myself in the house of Rimmon." I replied, "Go
in peace", and he departed.

Shortly thereafter, Gehazi went after him (2 Kings 5:20-
24). When he returned; he stood before me. I said to
him, "Where have you been, Gehazi?" He said, "I haven't
gone anywhere." I responded, "Did not my heart go with
you; when the man turned from his chariot to meet you?
Is it a time to receive money; clothes; olive groves and
vineyards; sheep and oxen, and male and female servants?
Therefore, the leprosy of Naaman shall cling to you and
your descendants forever." So, he went out a leper as white
as snow. I can't believe he was foolish enough to think
he could get away with a stunt like that. He got what he
deserved. I probably should not feel that way, but I do. This
is strange; I'm acting more and more like Elijah.

As time passed, things are going well. In fact; maybe a
little too well. We are running out of space at the house.
The sons of the prophets requested to build a bigger
house down by the Jordan. Of course, I gave my consent,
because like I said, we're running out of space. They also
requested that I go with them to oversee the project. So, we
all went down to the Jordan; picked a spot, and the men
start chopping down trees. Things seem to be progressing
marvelously; then one of the men came running to me in
a panic. He explained that he had lost the ax head, and to
make matters worse, the ax was borrowed. I told him to
show me where he was when the ax head came off. It had
gone into the river. I cut off a stick and tossed it into the
river. As soon as the stick hit the water the iron ax head
came floating to the top. I told the man to reach out and
pick up the ax head.

Here's a shocker for you. The king of Aram is plotting
another war. They have set up an ambush for the king

of Israel. So, I sent word to the king of Israel, be careful and avoid this place because Aram is waiting to ambush you there. After several failed attempts the king of Aram became enraged and inquired of his servants, "Tell me, which one of us is on the side of the king of Israel?" (2Kings 6:11) One of the servants spoke and said, "It's that prophet Elisha; who is telling the king of Israel all the words that are spoken in your bedroom." So, the king of Aram sent spies to find me. They found me in Dothan and returned a message to the king. He sent a large army to capture me. After surrounding the city at night, they waited 'til daybreak to capture me. Early in the morning my servant stepped outside and saw the Syrians surrounding the city. He came back inside in a panic saying, "What shall we do?" I replied, "Do not be afraid; those who are with us are more than those who are with them." (2Kings 6:16). Then I prayed, "O Lord, open his eyes so he can see what I see", and his eyes were opened and he saw the great army of chariots of fire on the hills.

As the Syrians attacked, I prayed, please strike these men with blindness, and it was so. When they reached the city; I told them, "This is not the way, and this is not the city. Follow me, and I will take you to the man you are seeking." Then I led them to Samaria. When we arrived at Samaria, I prayed, "O Lord open their eyes that they may see" and the men realized that they were in Samaria. When the king of Israel saw them; he inquired if he should kill them. The king of Israel was kind of shocked when I replied "Do not kill them. Would you kill those you have captured with your sword or bow? Set food and water before them, that they may eat and drink and then return to their master." The king did as I had commanded and sent the men back to Aram, and they never returned to the land of Israel again.

I promise you, the Syrians have to be the most hard-headed people on the planet. You would think by now, they would understand that going to war against Israel is going to end in disaster. Next up was Benhadad who assembled the armies of Aram and has come up to besiege Samaria. The siege lasted long enough to cause a famine in Samaria. Complaints began to mount before the king of Israel, and his frustrations mounted to the point where he made a proclamation; "May God punish me severely if the head of Elisha remains on his shoulders through this day!" I was sitting in my house with the elders, and the king sent a messenger ahead of himself. Before he arrived, I said to the elders, "Do you see how this murderer has sent someone to cut off my head? Look, when the messenger arrives, shut the door to keep him out." While I was still speaking with them, the messenger came to me, and said, "This calamity is from the LORD. Why should I wait for the LORD any longer?" I replied, "Hear the word of the LORD! This is what the LORD says: 'About this time tomorrow at the gate of Samaria, a seah (approx. 9 quarts) of fine flour will sell for a shekel (approx. 28 cents), and two seahs of barley will sell for a shekel.'" The king's right-hand man answered, "Unbelievable, could this happen? Even if the LORD were to make windows in heaven: it doesn't seem likely." My response to him was. "You will see it with your own eyes, but you will not eat any of it."

Meanwhile, there were four lepers at the gate of the city contemplating their lives (or the end thereof). They reasoned among themselves saying, "Why should we just sit here 'til we die?" They decided to take their chances and go to the Syrian camp. Upon arriving; they found the camp empty. The LORD had caused the Arameans to hear the sound of chariots, horses, and a great army, and they said to each other, "Look, the king of Israel must have hired the kings of the Hittites and Egyptians to attack us." (2Kings 7: 6) The lepers entered into the camp and found food; gold; silver, and clothes. They ate and drank, and carried off their spoils and hid them. Finally, they said to one another, "We are not doing what is right. Today is a day of good news. If we keep silent and wait until the morning; our sin will catch up with us. Now; therefore, let us go and tell the king. The lepers returned to the city and told the gatekeeper the news, who in turn, told the king. So the king sent spies to confirm the story told by the lepers. When it had been confirmed and told throughout the city; the people ran to the camp of the Arameans. In their haste; the stampede of people trampled the gatekeeper, and he died just as I had told him.

As time passed; I saw the Shunammite woman whose son I had restored to life, and I spoke unto her "You and your household need to go live as a foreigner wherever you can. The LORD has pronounced a seven-year famine, and it has already come to the land." So, the woman got ready and did as I instructed. They lived as foreigners for seven years in the land of the Philistines. At the end of seven years; the woman returned from the land of the Philistines. She went to the king to appeal on behalf of her house and her land. Now the king had been speaking to Gehazi, saying, "Please tell me all the great things Elisha has done." As Gehazi was telling the king how I brought the dead back to life; the woman whose son I had revived came to appeal to the king for her house and her land. So Gehazi said, "My lord the king; this is the woman; this is the son Elisha restored to life." When the king asked the woman if it was true; she confirmed it. So, the king appointed for her an officer saying, "Restore all that was hers, along with all the proceeds of the field from the day that she left the country until now."

After that, I went to Damascus while Ben-hadad king of Aram was sick, and the king was told, "The man of God has come here." So, the king said to Hazael, "Take a gift in your hands; go to meet the man of God, and request that he ask the Lord, 'Will I recover from this illness?'" So Hazael came to meet me; bringing a gift of forty camels loaded with everything that was good in Damascus. He stood in front of

me and said, "Your son Ben-hadad king of Aram has sent
me to ask, will he recover from this illness?" I answered,
"Go and tell him, 'You will certainly recover.' However; the
LORD has shown me that in fact, he will die." I fixed my
gaze steadily on him until Hazael became uncomfortable.
Then I began to weep. "Why are you weeping my lord?" he
asked. "Because I know the evil you will do to the people
of Israel," I responded. "You will set fire to their fortresses;
kill their young men with the sword; cut their little ones
to pieces, and rip open their pregnant women." "Are you
seriously kidding me? Am I a mere dog; that he would
do this monstrous thing?" Hazael said. I answered, "The
LORD has shown me that you will become king over Aram,
and as such; you will commit these horrific acts." So Hazael
left and returned to his master. Needless to say, Ben-hadad
got straight to the point and asked him, "What did Elisha
say to you?" He replied, "He told me you would surely
recover." The next day Hazael took a thick cloth; dipped it
in water; and spread it over Ben-hadad face. He died slowly
and painfully, and Hazael reigned in his place.

Some years after Ben-hadad's murder; I summoned one of
the sons of the prophets and said to him, "Tuck your cloak
under your belt; take this flask of oil, and go to Ramoth-
gilead. When you arrive; look for Jehu son of Jehoshaphat.
Go in; get him away from his companions, and take him
to an inner room. Then take the flask of oil; pour it on his
head, and declare, 'This is what the LORD says: I anoint
you king over Israel.' Then open the door and run. Do
not delay!" The young prophet did as he was instructed
(well, kind of). He found Jehu and anointed him; then
declared, "This is what the LORD God of Israel, says: 'I
anoint you king over My people, Israel. You are to strike
down the house of your master Ahab; so that I may avenge
the bloodshed by My servants, the prophets, and all the
servants of the LORD at the hand of Jezebel. The whole
house of Ahab will perish; I will cut off from Ahab; all the
males in Israel; both slave and free. I will make the house

of Ahab like the houses of Jeroboam and Baasha. The dogs will eat Jezebel on the plot of ground at Jezreel, and there will be no one to bury her.'" Then the young prophet opened the door and ran away.

This prophecy sent Jehu on a killing spree for the ages. Jehu set out for Jezreel; when he arrived at Naboth's property; Joram met him, and asked, "Have you come in peace, Jehu?" "As long as the idolatry and witchcraft of your mother Jezebel thrive; how can there be peace?" He replied. Joram attempted to flee; Jehu shot him in the back with an arrow, and he died. Jehu said to Bidkar his officer, "Pick him up and throw him into the field of Naboth the Jezreelite. Remember when you and I were riding together behind his father Ahab, and the LORD lifted this oracle against him? 'As surely as I saw the blood of Naboth and the blood of his sons yesterday; declared the LORD; so will I repay you on this plot of land.' Now then, according to the word of the LORD; pick him up and throw him on that plot of land." Having seen this; King Ahaziah he fled up the road toward Beth-haggan. Jehu pursued him; shouting "Shoot him too!" So, they shot Ahaziah in his chariot on the Ascent of Gur, and he fled to Megiddo and died.

Jehu then proceeded to Jezreel. When he arrived in Jezreel; Jezebel heard of it. She painted her eyes; adorned her head, and looked down from a window. As Jehu entered the gate, she asked, "Have you come in peace; the murderer of your master?" Jehu looked up at the window and called out, "Who is on my side?" The eunuchs looked down at him. "Throw her down!" So, they threw her down, and her blood splattered on the wall, and the horses as they trampled her underfoot. After that; Jehu went and ate and drank. "Take care of this cursed woman, and bury her, for she was the daughter of a king," he said. When the men went out to bury her; they found nothing but her skull; her feet, and the palms of her hands.

Later Jehu sent a letter to Samaria where Ahab's 70 sons were. The letter read, "When this letter arrives; since your master's sons are with you; you have chariots and horses; a fortified city and weaponry; select the best and most worthy son of your master. Set him on his father's throne, and fight for your master's house." Now they were terrified and reasoned among themselves, "If two kings could not stand against him; how can we?" So the elders; the palace administrator, the overseer of the city, and the guardians sent a message to Jehu: "We are your servants, and we will do whatever you say. Do whatever is good in your sight, but we will not make anyone king."

Jehu then wrote them a second letter and said: "If you are on my side, and if you will obey me; then bring the heads of your master's sons to me at Jezreel by this time tomorrow." Now the king's sons were being gathered up by the leading men of the city. When the letter arrived; they took the slaughtered king's sons; all seventy of them, and put their heads in baskets. Then a messenger arrived, and he told Jehu, "They have brought the heads of the king's sons." Then Jehu ordered, "Pile them in two heaps at the entrance of the gate until the morning." The next morning; Jehu went out and stood before all the people. He said, "You are innocent. I who conspired against my master and killed him, but who killed all these? Know this; not a word the LORD had spoken against the house of Ahab will fail. The LORD has done what He promised through His servant Elijah." Then Jehu killed everyone in Jezreel who remained of the house of Ahab; as well as all his great men; close friends and priests; leaving him without a single survivor.

Jehu met some relatives of Ahaziah king of Judah and asked, "Who are you?" "We are relatives of Ahaziah," they answered, "and we have come down to greet the sons of the king and queen mother." Then Jehu ordered, "Take them alive." His men took them alive; then slaughtered them at the well of Beth-eked; forty-two men in all. When he left there; he found Jehonadab son of Rechab; who was coming to meet him. Jehu greeted him and asked, "Are we like-minded, and on one accord?" "We are!" Jehonadab replied. "If we are; give me your hand," Jehu said. He gave him his hand, and Jehu helped him into his chariot, saying, "Come with me and see my zeal for the LORD!" When they arrived in Samaria; Jehu struck down everyone belonging to Ahab who remained there; according to the word that the LORD had spoken to Elijah.

Then Jehu brought all the people together and said, "Ahab served Baal a little, but Jehu will serve him a lot. Now, therefore; summon to me all the prophets of Baal, all his servants, and all his priests. See that no one is missing because I have a great sacrifice for Baal. Whoever is missing will not live." Then he commanded, "Proclaim a solemn assembly for Baal." and they called one. Then Jehu sent word throughout Israel, and all the servants of Baal came. They entered the temple of Baal, and it was full. Then Jehu said to the keeper of the wardrobe, "Bring out garments for all the servants of Baal." and he brought them out. Jehu and Jehonadab entered the temple of Baal, and Jehu said to the servants of Baal, "Look around to see that there are no servants of the LORD here among you." There were none, and they went in to offer sacrifices and burnt offerings. Now Jehu had stationed eighty men outside and warned them, "If anyone allows one person to escape; he will forfeit his life for theirs." When he had finished making the burnt offering; Jehu said to the guards and officers, "Go in and kill them. Do not let anyone out." So, the guards and officers struck them down with the sword; threw the bodies out, and went into the inner room of the temple of Baal. They brought out the sacred pillar of the temple of Baal and burned it. They demolished the sacred pillar of Baal; then they tore down the temple of Baal. They made it into a latrine, and it is to this day. However, Jehu did not turn away from the sins that Jeroboam had caused Israel to commit (the worship of the golden calves at Bethel and

Dan). Nevertheless, the LORD said to Jehu, "Because you have done well in carrying out what is right in My sight, and have done to the house of Ahab all that was in My heart; four generations of your sons will sit on the throne of Israel."

Now that everything associated with Ahab and Jezebel has been destroyed; my time is coming to an end. I have fallen sick with an illness from which I will not recover. Joash king of Israel came to visit me and wept over me. I told Joash; take a bow and some arrows; open the east window, and shoot! Joash did as commanded and I declared, "This is the LORD's arrow of victory; the arrow of victory over Aram. You shall strike the Arameans in Aphek until you have put an end to them." Then I said, "Take the arrows!" and strike the ground!" Joash struck the ground three times and stopped. I was furious with him and said, "You should have struck the ground five or six times. Then you would have struck down Aram until you had put an end to them, but now you will strike down Aram only three times." Not long after that; I died and was buried; one miracle shy of my double portion. Good thing I served a faithful God! He honored my initial request and my final miracle came after my death. Now the Moabite raiders would come into the land every spring. Once, as the Israelites were burying a man; they saw a band of raiders. They threw the man's body into my tomb. When his body touched my bones; the man was revived and stood up on his feet.

Jonah: Self-righteous or Arrogant

I know, every time you hear my name, most of you shake your heads. I'll bet; thoughts come to mind like why would he run from God? How did he think that was going to turn out? I promise you; I'm not the first person to be reluctant to do what God commanded. I guarantee you I'm not the last one either. In fact; how many of you, didn't want to accept your calling?

My life was perfectly fine, then one day the Lord said, "Arise! Go to that great city of Nineveh and preach against it, because its wickedness has come up before Me." I wanted to say, "Absolutely NOT! But I figured that wouldn't go over so well. I mean, why should I go to Nineveh? As wicked as those people are; they deserve to feel the wrath of God. So, I got up and fled from the presence of the LORD. I went down to Joppa and found a ship bound for Tarshish. I paid the fare and went to the bottom of the ship and went to sleep. Then the LORD sent a violent wind upon the sea, and a violent storm arose so that the ship was in danger of breaking apart. The sailors were afraid, and each one cried out to his god. Then, they threw the ship's cargo into the sea to lighten the load. The captain woke me and said, "How can you sleep? Get up and call upon your God. Perhaps this God will hear you, and spare our lives."

The sailors said to one another, "Let us cast lots to find out who is responsible for this calamity." We cast lots, and the lot fell on me. So, they wanted to know who I was, where I'm from, and what nationality I am. "I am a Hebrew," I replied. "I worship the LORD, the God of the heavens, who made the sea and the dry land." The storm grew worse, so they asked, "What must we do to you to calm this sea?" I replied. "Pick me up and cast me into the sea.

Then it will calm down for you. I know that I am to blame for this violent storm that has come upon us." They were hesitant to do so, and the men began to row harder to get back to dry land. It was a lesson in futility. The harder they rowed; the less progress was made, because the sea was raging against them. Then the men cried out to the LORD: "Please, O LORD, do not let us perish on account of this man's life! Do not put innocent blood on us! For You, O LORD, have done as You pleased." Then they picked me up and threw me into the sea, and the storm ceased. As soon as I hit the water a great fish swallowed me, and I spent three days and three nights in the stomach of that fish.

When I was swallowed by the great fish, it was kind of interesting, but when reality set in, it became increasingly terrifying. It's dark, damp and quite smelly in there. Miraculously, I was not being digested in that belly, but on the other hand, I was not in a mindset to marvel at the miraculous. Once I realized the gravity of my predicament, I called out to the Lord and prayed. "In my distress, I called to the LORD and He answered me. From the belly of hell, I called for help, and You heard my voice. For You cast me into the deep, into the heart of the seas, and the currents swirled about me. I said, 'I have been banished from Your sight, yet I will look once more toward Your holy temple.' As my life was fading away, I remembered the LORD. My prayer went up to You, to Your holy temple. With the voice of thanksgiving, I will sacrifice to You. I will fulfill what I have vowed. Salvation is from the LORD!" Then the Lord commanded the fish, and it vomited up onto dry land.

Not long after, the word of the Lord came to me again. "Arise! Go to the great city of Nineveh and proclaim the message that I will give you." This time, I did as God commanded and went to Nineveh. The city is huge, it will take three days to cross. I proclaimed a simple message. In 40 days, God will destroy this city. The Ninevites believed

God. They proclaimed a fast and dressed in sackcloth. The word reached the king, and he got up from his throne, took off his royal robe, covered himself with sackcloth, and sat in ashes. He issued a proclamation in the city: "By the decree of the king and his nobles: Let no man or beast, herd nor flock, taste anything at all. They must not eat or drink. Also, let both man and beast be covered with sackcloth, and have everyone call out earnestly to God. Let each one turn from his evil ways and the violence in his hands. Maybe, just maybe, this will cause God to change His mind and spare us from His impending wrath. When God saw their actions, how they turned from their wicked ways, He did change His mind and spared the city.

Normally, this would make a preacher extremely happy. Just think a simple message like the one I delivered in Nineveh, and the entire city turned from its wickedness and was saved. What a mighty God! This, however, was not the case. I was very angry, and called out to God. "See this is the very reason why I didn't want to come to Nineveh, to begin with. The last time, a city was this wicked, you wiped it out. You didn't even spare them at Abraham's request. When you gave Moses the law in the wilderness, you said all idolaters would be destroyed. Now here we are, and you have decided to spare Nineveh because they turned from their wicked ways. In the back of my mind, I knew this was going to happen, and that's why I went to Tarshish. Now, you might as well take my life, it's better for me to die, than to live." Then the Lord asked, "Why are you angry?" I left the city and sat down east of it, where I built a shelter and sat down and pouted. Then God provided a vine, and it grew up to provide shade for me to ease my grief, and I was very happy with the plant. The next morning, God sent a worm to eat the vine, and it withered. As the sun rose, God sent a very hot east wind; the sun beat down on my head, I grew faint, and wished to die, saying, "It is better for me to die than to live." Then God asked, "Have you any right to be angry about the plant?" "I do," I replied. "I am angry enough to die!" The LORD said, "You cared about the plant, which you neither grew nor tended. It sprang up in a night and perished in a night. So, should I not care about the great city of Nineveh, which has more than 120,000 people who cannot tell their right hand from their left"

Well, at least my attitude didn't get me killed, so I guess that is a good thing, but I knew that God wasn't at all pleased with it.

Thomas: Misunderstood or Rightly Judged

It is said, don't criticize a person, unless you've walked in his/her shoes.

My name is Thomas and you like to refer to me as "Doubting Thomas". Jesus, never called me that, nor did my fellow apostles, so, why should you? Some even incorrectly think that my surname Didymus means doubter, but in reality, it means twin. Why do you choose to judge me so harshly? We all have flaws and have doubted things we've been told by others. We all know pranksters; habitual liars; drama queens; pessimists, and con artists. The longer we interact with these people, the more difficult it becomes to believe what they say. Call me cynical, but if you think about it, you'll come to the same conclusion. Do any of you label yourselves as doubters? Let's examine this naturally and spiritually.

I was one of the chosen disciples/apostles. As you know there were twelve of us, and one was a devil (John 6.70). We'll get to that later. Let's look at the cast of characters we're dealing with here and maybe, just maybe you'll understand my position. I spent 3 ½ years with these guys. Upfront and personal years, no hiding, all character flaws exposed. Here's what I was dealing with.

Matthew was a tax collector, no one more crooked and dishonest during that period than a tax collector. In my time, tax collectors would even steal from their mothers. To say they were a hated group of individuals might be an understatement. Jesus clearly saw something in this man, that we didn't. Trusting him took a lot of effort.

Luke was a physician, very intelligent, but slightly on the

self-absorbed side. You know the type: always has the answers; always comes to the "logical conclusion"; finds it difficult to think outside the box.

HA! Speaking of self-absorbed, we have James and John (the sons of Zebedee), who think nothing is wrong with their mother requesting of Jesus that one sit at His right hand and the other at His left. John was also very ambitious and had quite the temper. Not to mention Jesus gave them the name Boanerges (Mark 3:17), which the Greeks mistranslate bene reghes, "sons of thunder". In actuality, the original Hebrew ben regaz, "sons of rage". There was an incident one day while traveling through Samaria and some of the villagers didn't want us staying there. James and John wanted to call down fire from heaven (Luke 9:54). That was a bit extreme, but that's the way they were at times.

Judas the Zealot (Thaddeus) was a bit radical, his solution to every problem was to fight. He felt that the Jews shouldn't be tolerating Roman occupation. He felt that Jesus should reveal Himself as a ruling king.

Simon Peter, ah, what a character indeed. He was impulsive; hot-headed; stubborn; a liar, and would cuss you out if you made him mad. He was insightful one minute and spiritually blind the next. This man jumped out of the boat to walk on water. He cut off an ear of one of the men that showed up to arrest Jesus. He told Jesus he was willing to die for him but lied 3 times to save himself. He even cussed a girl out in the process.

That brings us to Judas Iscariot, the one whom Jesus called a devil. He was greedy; still trying to figure out how we let him keep the purse. His betrayal is most famous and his suicide equally as infamous. The personalities of the others were not recorded biblically, so I won't attempt to muddy the waters by giving you my impression of them.

Now let's go through the events as they happened.

Throughout Jesus' 3 ½ yrs. of ministry, we have been
rebuked many times for our unbelief, our lack of faith, and
for our lack of insight into spiritual matters. Of course, no
one likes to be rebuked, but I will admit; most of the time
we deserved it. My most memorable moment was when
we were out on the sea at night and it was very windy
and the sea was rough. Here comes Jesus walking on the
water and needless to say we're about to lose our minds
because we didn't realize it was Him. We all thought it was
a ghost. Then all of a sudden, Mr. Impulsive (Peter) cries
out, "Lord if it is you, bid me come to you on the water."
Jesus said, "Come". I don't know about you, but getting out
of that boat was not my first choice. Needless to say, we
were shocked when this crazy man seriously climbed out
of the boat. We were even more shocked when he actually
started walking on the water! All I could think was, he'll
never make it. Honestly, closer to the truth is he better not
make it, because we'll never hear the end of it. About the
time Peter is within a few steps from Jesus he looks around
and got scared. He started to sink like a rock, and I said to
myself, "I knew he wasn't going to make it". We all sighed
a sigh of relief. About that time Jesus reached out and
grabbed Peter by the hand to save him. Jesus said, "O ye of
little faith, wherefore, did you DOUBT?" (Matt 14.31)

Fast forward to the day of Jesus' arrest. We are having
supper and Jesus is reiterating His need to die and reveals
Judas' betrayal. After supper, we sang a song and went to
the Mount of Olives. Jesus reveals after His death we'll run
and hide for fear, and Mr. Impulsive sticks his foot in his
mouth again, and starts talking about everyone else may
hide, but I won't. Jesus gently shook His head and replied,
"Before the cock crows, you will have denied knowing
me three times." Sure enough, Jesus was being mocked
and beaten and as we watched from a distance, someone
recognized Peter. They questioned him and just as Jesus

117

said, Peter denied knowing Him and even cussed a lady out. When the cock crowed; Peter hung his head in shame and ran away.

Fast forward to resurrection morning, Mary and some of the women went to the tomb and encounter two angels. They told Mary to go tell us (the disciples) and even singled Peter out, that Jesus has risen and He will meet us in Galilee. Some of the disciples had heard that Jesus was alive, and had been seen by Mary, but didn't believe it (Mark 16.11). The rest of the disciples were told and they didn't believe it either (Mark 16.13). In fact, we all went back to our former occupations.

That same day; there were two disciples on their way to Emmaus. As they walked; they encountered Jesus, but they didn't realize it was Him. As they talked Jesus said, "O fools and slow of heart to believe all that the prophets have spoken..." (Luke 24.25-6) They convinced the man to stay with them for a while, and they ate a meal. It wasn't until the man took the bread and blessed it, and gave it to them, that they knew it was Jesus. Then He vanished. When the two disciples returned to Jerusalem; they told the others what happened. While they told their story; Jesus appeared in front of them. Now, everybody, there was scared to death; thinking they were seeing a spirit. He showed them His hands and His side. (Luke 24.36-40, John 20.20). Even after several different encounters with Jesus; none of them didn't believe it was Him. I wasn't there to witness any of this. (John 20.24)

So now it comes down to everyone who has seen Jesus after His resurrection except for me. Take into account everything that has happened; I know these people personally; I've shown you biblically where they had seen Jesus, and didn't believe it until He proved Himself. Now the time comes when everyone is telling me that Jesus has risen, and they have seen Him. I'm sorry, but I'm not going to just take their word for it. So, I merely ask to do the very thing; the rest of them have already done. I want to see the wounds for myself. (John 20:25) About a week later (eight days to be exact); we were all together and Jesus appeared before us. He greeted us and told me to come to touch His wounds. That was not necessary; I knew it was Him when He stretched out His hands. I said "My Lord and my God". Jesus replied, "Thomas, you believe because you have seen. Blessed are they that believe, and have not seen". I learned a very valuable lesson that day; getting proof is easy, but faith not so much!

Peter: Polished Yet Still Rough

Everything that glitters ain't gold, and even a polished diamond has edges that can cut. I should know, I had my share of rough edges. Truth be told, I probably had more than my share of rough edges. By the time I finish telling you my story, you may wonder if I ever completely got rid of them. I can promise you that the majority of them have ceased to cut.

The day starts like most any other day with one minor exception. My brother Andrew, and I had been fishing all night long and came home empty handed. Needless to say, it was a frustrating night. We're on the shore of Lake Gennesaret cleaning our nets, getting ready for another day. Then I noticed that some guy had gotten into my boat, and set out a little way off the shore. I said, "what the (expletive deleted)?" I ran to the water's edge to confront him and give him a piece of my mind, but I couldn't. I really want to interrupt him while he's speaking to a crowd of people, but there's something about him; I can't quite put my finger on it, but something in his eyes had this great calming effect on me. His voice was powerful; it penetrated my soul and drew me in. When he was finished talking to the crowd, he said, "Simon, launch out into the deep and let down your nets for a haul." Now I know he's not from around here. Nobody calls me Simon! I replied, "Master, we have worked all night and caught nothing; nevertheless, at your word we will do it." We launched out into the deep part of the lake and let down a net. Within seconds something was pulling on the net. Andrew and I struggled to pull them in. Then we realized the net was full nearly to the point of breaking. Don't look at me like that. I know I didn't follow His instructions to the letter. Had I done so; we wouldn't be tearing up our net right now. By the way, how many times have you been given instructions that you didn't follow to the letter? Exactly! I called out to James and John, the sons of Zebedee for help. We filled both boats to the point of nearly sinking. I'm thinking to myself; this is crazy!! We were just out in this area and caught nothing. How is this possible? Then it dawned on me, this must be Jesus, whom everyone is talking about. I bowed myself to His knees and said, "Walk away from me LORD, because I am a sinful man." Jesus replied, "Don't be afraid Simon, I will make you a fisher of men."

After we reached the shore, Andrew, James, John, and I left everything behind and followed Jesus. The next day Jesus saw Phillip and said, "Follow me." How does He do that? The simplicity of how He deals with people. I'm going to have to figure this out. The next few days there were a series of jaw dropping events. I mean the things that we witnessed: astonishing might even be an understatement. A man with leprosy walked right up to Jesus. You know according to the law that God gave to Moses; such a thing was not only forbidden; it was punishable by death. He said, "LORD, if you are willing, you can make me clean." Jesus didn't even flinch. He reached out and touched the leper and said, "I am willing, be clean." Instantly the man's leprosy was gone! Jesus told him to tell no one what he had done; just go show himself to the priest. Next, we went to my mother-in-law's house and he healed her of her sickness. Then there was a man who was paralyzed. His friends could not get into the house through either door; so they climbed up on the roof and tore it off and lowered their friend down on the stretcher at Jesus's feet. When He looked up and saw their faith, He said, "Friend, your sins are forgiven you." Now that infuriated the Pharisees, and they accused him of blasphemy. He knew what they were thinking, and He asked, "Is it easier to say; your sins are forgiven, or arise take up your bed and walk?" He continued on, "That you may know that the Son of Man has power on Earth to forgive sins; arise take up your bed and go home." Immediately; the man picked up his bed and went home glorifying God. Next a centurion came up to Jesus, and let Him know that his servant was sick and in agony. Jesus told him that he would go to his house, but the centurion said, "I am not worthy. Just speak the word and I know he will be healed." Jesus replied, "I have not seen this much faith in all of Israel. Go your way, as you believe, so shall it be done." When I tell you Jesus is cool under pressure, I mean nothing phases Him. Nothing is too difficult; nothing is too strange. He healed all kinds of diseases. He even talked to demons and they obeyed His commands.

Unlike most nights, tonight is different. Jesus has gone up into the mountains. In the morning He came back down and gathered those of us that have followed Him continually. He chose twelve of us to become His apostles. He chose myself; my brother Andrew; James and John the sons of Zebedee; Philip; Bartholomew; Matthew; Thomas; James son of Alphaeus; Simon called the Zealot; Judas son of James, and Judas Iscariot. Then Jesus began to teach the crowd using parables, and when we were alone, He would tell us their meanings. On this particular day, when He finished teaching, He sent the crowd away, and we went down to the shore and got into the boat. We set out for the other side of the lake and Jesus had gone to the back of the ship to sleep. Suddenly a great storm came out of nowhere and ship began to toss to and fro. We were taking on water and we were getting scared. Remember when I said Jesus was cool? There He is, in the back of the boat fast asleep. He looks so peaceful, but He's way too peaceful and we're about to be torn apart by this storm. In a bit of a panic, we woke Him up and said, "Master don't you care that we are about to die?" Jesus shook His head and stood up. He spoke to the storm and said., "Peace: be still!" Immediately the winds stopped, and the waves stopped crashing against the boat. Again, we were awe struck and wondered among ourselves saying, "What kind of man is this, that even the wind obeys Him?" He then turned to us and said, "Why were you so afraid? How is it; that you have no faith?"

Today is like any other day. Large crowds of people trying to get to Jesus so they can be healed, delivered, blessed. Well, maybe I was wrong. This crowd is more aggressive than others have been. Actually, this was getting annoying. People pushing and pulling, trying to get their hands on Jesus. All of a sudden, He turned around and asked, who touched His clothes. You can't be serious!! All these people pushing and pulling, reaching out to touch Him and He asked, "Who touched Me?" We all chimed in simultaneously, "You can see the crowd pressing in on You, and You ask, 'Who touched Me?" Jesus kept looking around. Then a woman came up to Him and fell at His feet. She told Him her story. He said to her, "Daughter, your faith has made you whole. Go in peace and be free of your affliction."

The time came when Jesus sent us out to testify of God's glory and to do many things. We cast out devils; healed the sick; opened blind eyes; we returned to Jesus rejoicing. We were joyous, having preformed all the same miracles that He had done. We were comparing notes, as if it were a competition. Jesus said, "I have given you authority over all the power of the enemy, but don't rejoice because demons are subject to you. Rejoice that your names are written in Heaven." Now trust me; as great as it was to have demons afraid of us; we had a few embarrassing moments also. Like the time Jesus was explaining how He would be rejected by the elders and scribes. I rebuked Him saying, "That will never happen." Boy was that ever a huge mistake. Jesus whirled around and said to me, "Get behind me Satan. You don't have a mind for the things of God." Wait; He just called me Satan. That was a bit harsh. Well, maybe not. I shouldn't have overstepped my bounds.

Then there was that time when Jesus was walking on water (for the second time). You would have thought we had learned our lesson the first time. I don't know what it is that makes Him want to walk on the water at night. That's just creepy, but I digress. Anyway! We're trying to cross the sea and the wind is howling. Next thing you know, we see this figure approaching. We were terrified, we were screaming and yelling, then we heard this voice saying, "Don't be afraid, It's Me." That's not very comforting to some of us, but me; I said, "If it is you Jesus, bid me to come to you on the water." He said, "Come." I climbed out of the boat, and the others thought I had lost my mind. After a few steps I said to the others, "I told you it was Him" I was almost to Jesus and the wind picked up. The water splashed against my ankles, and I started looking around. I lost focus on Jesus and I sank. I panicked; not quite sure why. I'm a fisherman; I know how to swim. While I floundered about in the water; I cried out, "Jesus, save me!" Jesus reached out and grabbed me by the hand. He said, "Your faith is small! Why did you doubt?" We walked back to the boat. After we had climbed back into it; the wind ceased. The look on the others' faces can only mean one thing: I'm not going to live this down anytime soon.

We continue to grow in knowledge and in grace. Jesus has taught us a lot of things. He also continued to speak of His betrayal and death. The miracles continued. The crowds of people continued to grow. Jesus has fed the multitudes twice. He raised Lazarus from the dead when it should have been impossible. According to Jewish customs; the soul of a person is believed to linger in this realm for three days. Then it returned to God. Lazarus was dead four. This in and of itself should have proven Jesus' divinity, but it did not. One day, while walking along the coast of Caesarea Philippi, Jesus asked us whom people thought He was. We answered, John the Baptist, Elijah, Jerimiah, or one of the other prophets. Then He said, "Whom do you say that I am?" I blurted out, "You are the Christ; the son of the Living God!" Jesus replied, "It is upon this revelation, that I will build my church, and the gates of Hell, will not prevail against it." Unfortunately, we vacillated between knowing who Jesus was, to having no clue at all.

Once again, Jesus talked to us about His need to die at the hands of sinful men. We are headed to Jerusalem to prepare for Passover. We entered the city with fanfare fit for a king. In this atmosphere, it's hard to imagine that Jesus could ever be betrayed. Jesus continued teaching, both in the streets and in the temple. He spoke in parables, but the priests and the scribes knew He was talking about them. They were angry and began to plot against Him. The Pharisees and Sadducees attempted to trap Him with questions so they would have something to accuse Him of that was worthy of imprisonment. They failed at every turn. Jesus called them hypocrites and fools. Needless to say; they were furious. So, Jesus had managed to upset every religious leader with His teachings, and they wanted Him in prison. They wanted Him dead!

One night we were all assembled in an upper room and Jesus began to reiterate the circumstance of His death. Everyone wanted to know who would betray Jesus. He responded, "Whoever dips his hand in the dish with Me; he is the one who will betray Me." So, now we really can't wait to see who the traitor is. Kind of hard to believe that after all that we've been a part of, that someone would actually do such a thing. Jesus continued on saying that we would run away from Him when He was taken. I said, "No way, I'll never leave your side." The others chimed in as well. Jesus replies to me, "Before the cock crows, you will deny me three times." "Not so LORD", I replied, "Even if it means dying; I will never deny you." Then we sang a song and went out to the Mount of Olives.

We got to Gethsemane, and Jesus told us, "Sit here while I go over there and pray." He took me, James, and John into the garden. He said, "I am extremely sorrowful, even unto death: wait here, and watch with me. Then Jesus went a little further into the garden. After a while we fell asleep. Jesus came back and found us sleeping. He woke us up, and said to me, "Could you not wait with me one hour? Watch and pray that you do not fall into temptation. The spirit is willing, but the flesh is weak." Then Jesus went back and prayed some more. Again, He came back and found us sleeping. He woke us up; little did we know that this was His third time. He said, "The hour is at hand and the Son of Man is being betrayed into the hands of sinners. We walked out of the garden to where the rest of the disciples were waiting; while Judas was approaching with a large crowd. He walked up and kissed Jesus. Immediately, some of the men grabbed Him. I pulled out a knife and cut of an ear of one of the guys that grabbed Jesus. Jesus rebuked me and said, "Put away your knife, he that draws a sword, will die by the sword. I don't need you to defend me. I could ask my Father, and He would send down 12 legions of angels to defend Me." They arrested Jesus and just as He said, we all scattered.

I followed Jesus from a distance to Caiaphas' house. I sat down in the courtyard and watched things unfold. Several people came before the high priest and accused Jesus falsely. Jesus didn't say a word. There's a whole lot of commotion going on; can't quite figure out what though. Next thing I know; this girl came up to me and said, "You were with Jesus." "No, you have me confused with someone else." I walked away from her and walked toward the gate. Then another girl walked up to me and said loudly, "This man was with Jesus of Nazareth." Girl, I promise you, I don't know that man", I replied. After a little while, some of the people standing near me said, "We know you're one of them, because your speech betrays you." "Expletive, expletive deleted." I swear; I don't know that man; expletive deleted." Immediately, the cock crowed, and I felt an overwhelming sense of guilt come over me. I remembered what Jesus said and I ran out of the courtyard, and wept bitterly! How did I get to this place? How is it possible that I can have a revelatory experience and blurt out, "You are the Christ": to now lying that I even now Him. I'm beginning to understand why Jesus said my faith was small. My need for self-preservation just caused me to make the most devastating mistake of my life. How am I going to live with myself? Can I live with myself?

I witnessed the crucifixion of Jesus from a distance and the guilt is still with me. The sun hid its face and the Earth shook violently at His death. The crowd dispersed and His body was removed from the cross. His body was laid in a tomb and a boulder placed at the mouth of it. It's over; all hope is gone; I have no clue what I'm going to do. It's hard to believe or imagine how much shame I'm feeling.

On the first day of the week, Mary told a group of us that she had been to the tomb and Jesus had risen. At first, I didn't believe her; honestly; none of us did. I needed to see for myself. I went to the tomb and His body was definitely gone. However, the angel that Mary said met her at the tomb was nowhere to be found. It didn't take long for the Pharisees to say that someone took the body and hid it. Well, I don't know about anyone else, but I'm going fishing. Later on, two of the men that had followed Jesus, told us that they had talked with Jesus on the road to Emmaus. We didn't believe them either. About that time, Jesus appeared before us. We were all scared to death, thinking we had seen a spirit. Jesus immediately rebuked us saying, "Why are you terrified, and why do doubt in your hearts? Look at My hands and My feet. Touch Me and see. A spirit does not have flesh and bones." Everyone was present except for Thomas, and we couldn't wait to tell him that we have seen Jesus for ourselves. Later that day when Thomas arrived, we told him of our encounter. He didn't believe us, and honestly, I can't say that I blame him. None of us believed the news of his resurrection; except for Mary, until we saw the nail prints in His hands and feet for ourselves. Eight days later, Thomas got his wish. We're all together in the house with the door locked, and Jesus appeared before us. He said, "Peace be with you." Then He said to Thomas, "Put your finger into My hands. Reach out and put your hand into My side."

The next time Jesus appeared before us was on the shore at Tiberias. We shared a meal together, and when we were finished eating, He said to me, "Peter, do you love me more than these?" "You know I love You", I replied. He said, "Feed My lambs." Then He asked a second time, "Peter, do you love Me?" I said, "Yes LORD, You know I love You." He said, "Tend to My sheep." Jesus then asked a third time, "Peter, do you love me?" Now my feelings are hurt, because He felt the need to ask me the same question three times. I said, "LORD you know all things. You know I really do love You." He said, "Feed my sheep." Finally, a release; the pressure I was feeling is gone. Better still; the guilt is gone! I now understand the restorative and transformative power of forgiveness. I feel like Jesus has just placed His seal of approval on my life, and I have a new outlook.

So just before He ascended into Heaven for the las time, Jesus told us to remain in Jerusalem until we receive the gift that was promised. He said, "You will receive power when the Holy Spirit comes upon you; You will be My witnesses in Jerusalem; in all Judea and Samaria, and to the ends of the Earth." We all stayed in the upper room. In unity we all continued in prayer along with the women and Mary the mother of Jesus, and with His brothers. I stood among the brothers (about 120 in all), and said "Brothers, the scripture had to be fulfilled; the Holy Spirit proclaimed through the mouth of David concerning Judas, who became a guide for those who arrested Jesus. He was one of our number and shared in this ministry. Since he is no longer with us, it is necessary to select one of the men who has accompanied us, while the LORD Jesus was with us. After praying about it, we chose Matthias. On the day of Pentecost, we were assembled together in unity in the upper room. Suddenly, there came a sound from Heaven like a rushing mighty wind, and it filled the whole house. There appeared to be cloven tongues of fire, and it sat upon each of us. We were filled with the Holy Ghost, and began to speak in other tongues as the Spirit allowed. When this noise was heard, a crowd gathered. They were confused, because every man heard them speak in his own language. The people in the crowd began to at ask, "Are not all these men who are speaking Galileans? How is it that each of us hear them in our own language? What does this mean?" Other people in the crowd mocked us saying, "These men are drunk on new wine!"

Hearing their mockery, I stood up with the eleven and proclaimed, "Men of Judea and all who dwell in Jerusalem; we are not drunk like you think. It is only the third hour! What you are witnessing, was prophesied by the prophet Joel. 'In the last days,' God says, 'I will pour out My Spirit on all people. Your sons and daughters will prophesy; your young men will see visions; your old men will dream dreams. I will show wonders in the heavens. I will show signs on the earth; blood and fire and billows of smoke. The sun will be turned to darkness, and the moon to blood, before the coming of the LORD. Everyone who calls on the name of the LORD will be saved.' Men of Israel, hear me, and hear me well! You know Jesus of Nazareth was a man proven by God to you by miracles, wonders and signs which God did among you through Him. He was delivered up by you, and by the hands of the lawless according to the foreknowledge of God. You put Him to death by nailing Him to the cross, and God has raised up. He released Him from the pains of death, because it was not possible for death to hold Him. God raised this Jesus to life, and we are all witnesses. He was exalted to the right hand of God; received from the Father the promised Holy Spirit, and has poured out what you now see and hear. Therefore, let all Israel know with certainty, that God has made this same

Jesus, whom you crucified, both LORD and Christ!" Then the people were sorrowful and asked, "Brothers, what shall we do?" I replied, "Repent and be baptized, every one of you, in the name of Jesus Christ for the remission of your sins, and you will receive the gift of the Holy Ghost. This promise belongs to you and to your children, and to all who are far off; to all whom the LORD our God will call." Then those that gladly received the message were baptized. There were about three thousand souls added unto them. We continued to meet daily in the temple courts; we shared meals from house to house with gladness and sincerity of heart. We praised God and enjoyed the favor of all the people, and the LORD added to our numbers daily.

One afternoon, John and I were going to the temple at the hour of prayer. A man who was lame from birth was being carried to the gate called Beautiful, where he was sat every day begging. When he saw us about to enter the temple, he asked us for money. We looked at him, and I said, "Look at us!" He looked at us expecting to receive some money. I said, "I do not have silver or gold, but what I do have, I'll give you. In the name of Jesus Christ of Nazareth, get up and walk!" I took him by the right hand, and immediately the man's feet and ankles were strengthened. Leaping up he stood, and walked. We entered into the temple walking. Then he started leaping, and praising God. When the people saw him leaping and praising God, they recognized him as the man who used to sit begging at the gate of the temple. They were amazed at what had happened. I said, "Men of Israel, why are you surprised by this? Why do you stare at us as if we made this man walk by our own power? God has glorified His son Jesus, whom you rejected; then handed Him over to Pilate, despite his desire to release Him. You rejected the Holy and Righteous One and asked for a murderer to be released. You killed the Creator of life. God raised Him from the dead, and we were witnesses of that fact. By faith in the name of Jesus this man has been made strong. By that alone has he been given this complete healing in your presence." Many who heard the message believed, and there was about five thousand added to the church.

While John and I were speaking to the people; the priests; the captain of the temple guard, and the Sadducees came up to us. They were very troubled that we were teaching the people, and proclaiming the resurrection Jesus from the dead. They took us into custody until the next day. They brought us before the rulers; elders; scribes; Annas the high priest, and Caiaphas. They began to question us, "By what authority or what name did you do this?" Then I, being full of the Holy Ghost, said to them, "Rulers and elders of the people! Are we being interrogated today about a kind deed to a man who was lame? Are you trying to determine how he was healed? Then let this be known to all of you: it is by the name of Jesus Christ of Nazareth, whom you crucified, and God raised from the dead, that this man stands before you healed. He is the stone you builders rejected, and has become the cornerstone. There is salvation in no one else, because there is no other name under heaven, given to men, whereby we can be saved." When they saw our boldness and realized that we were ordinary men, they were impressed and took note that we had been with Jesus. We were ordered to leave the Sanhedrin and then they deliberated together. They called us back in and commanded us not to speak or teach in the name of Jesus. We replied, "Judge for yourselves whether it is right in God's sight to listen to you or to God. We cannot stop speaking about what we have seen and heard." Then the Council members threatened us further and let us go. They could not find a way to punish us, because the people were glorifying God for what had happened. With great power, we continued to give our testimony about the resurrection of the LORD Jesus. His abundant grace was upon all of us.

Those who owned lands or houses sold their property,

brought the proceeds to us, and we distributed it to anyone that had a need. Joseph, a Levite from Cyprus, whom we called Barnabas (Son of Encouragement), sold a field he owned. He brought the money, and laid it at our feet. Then Ananias, with his wife Sapphira, also sold a piece of land. With his wife's full knowledge, he kept back some of the proceeds for himself. He brought a portion and laid it at our feet. I asked, "Ananias, how is it that Satan has filled your heart to lie to the Holy Ghost? You have withheld some of the proceeds from the land. It was yours to sell, and after it was sold, wasn't the money at your disposal? How could you conceive such a deed in your heart? You have not lied to men, but to God!" After hearing these words, Ananias fell dead, and great fear came over everyone who heard what had happened. Then the young men stepped forward, wrapped up his body, and carried him out and buried him. About three hours later his wife came in, unaware of what had happened. I asked her, "Is this the price you and your husband got for the land?" "Yes," she answered, "that is it." I shook my head. "How could you agree to test the Holy Ghost?" I replied. "Look, the men who buried your husband are at the door, and they will carry you out also." Immediately she died. The young men came in and found her dead. So, they carried her out and buried her beside her husband. Great fear came over the whole church and everyone who heard about these events. More and more believers were brought to the LORD, both men and women.

As a result, people brought the sick into the streets and laid them on cots and mats, so that at least my shadow might fall on some of them as I passed by. Crowds also gathered from the towns around Jerusalem, bringing the sick and those tormented by unclean spirits, and all of them were healed. Then the high priest and all the Sadducees were jealous. They arrested us and put them in the common prison. During the night an angel of the LORD opened the doors of the prison. He said, "Go, stand in the temple courts and tell the people the full message of this new life." At daybreak, we entered the temple courts and began to teach the people. Not long after, the captain of the temple guard came with the officers and took us. It was not by force; however, because they feared the people would stone them. We stood before the Sanhedrin, and the high priest interrogated us. He said, "Didn't we give you strict orders not to teach in this name? Yet you have filled all Jerusalem with your teaching, and you are determined to make us responsible for this man's blood." The apostles and I replied, "We must obey God rather than men. The God of our fathers raised up Jesus, whom you had killed by hanging Him on a tree. God exalted Him to His right hand as Prince and Savior; in order to grant repentance and forgiveness of sins to Israel. We are witnesses of these things, and so is the Holy Ghost."

When the Council members heard this, they were outraged and wanted to put us to death. Then Gamaliel, a teacher of the law, and a Pharisee who was honored by all the people, stood up in the Sanhedrin and ordered us to go outside for a short time. They called us back inside and had us beaten. Then they ordered us not to speak in the name of Jesus, and released us. We left the Sanhedrin, rejoicing that we had been counted worthy to suffer for His name. We did not stop teaching and proclaiming the good news that Jesus is the Christ. Every day, we went to the temple courts and from house to house.

One day, I went to the rooftop of Simon's house to pray. As I was praying, I had a vision. There was what appeared to be a sheet descending from heaven. When it came to rest on the roof, it unfolded and it contained all manner of four-footed animals. There were wild beasts, creeping things, and birds. Then a voice said, "Peter, get up and eat." "Absolutely not! I have never eaten anything unclean, and I'm not going to start now." I replied. The voice spoke a second time. "Peter, get up and eat!" I said, "There is NO way I'm eating any of this. I have not, nor will I ever eat anything that is unclean." Maybe I shouldn't have said that. You know that tone of voice a parent has while scolding a child? Well, that voice replied in that tone, "What God has cleaned, don't you call it common." This happened a third time, and then the sheet was taken back into heaven. After the vision was over, I was confused as to it's meaning. Why would an angel, or God, or whomever that voice belonged to tell me to go against my own custom? About that time, there was a commotion outside the gate, and another voice spoke to me and said, "Get up, go downstairs and accompany these me without hesitation, because I have sent them." I did as I was told. I greeted the men and asked why they were here. "Cornelius the centurion has sent us," they said. "He is a righteous and God-fearing man with a good reputation among the Jews. A holy angel instructed him to request your presence in his home; so he could hear a message from you." I invited them in to stay the night, and the next day we set out to Caesarea.

A day later we were at the house of Cornelius to find he had gathered his family and close friends. Cornelius met us at the door and fell at my feet to worship me, but I helped him up saying, "Stand up sir, I am just a man like you." I continued on, "You know it is unlawful for a Jew to associate with a foreigner or visit him, but God has shown me that I am not to call or consider any of you common. So, when you invited me, I came without objection. Why have you sent for me?" Cornelius answered: "Four days ago, I was praying at the ninth hour. Suddenly an angel of the LORD stood before me, and said, 'Cornelius, your prayer has been heard, and your gifts to the poor have been remembered by God. Send for Simon, who is called Peter. He is a guest in the home of Simon the Tanner, in Joppa.' So, I sent for you immediately. Now, we are here in the presence of God to listen to everything the LORD has instructed you to tell us."

Then Peter began to speak: "Now I fully understand that God is not a respecter of persons, but welcomes everyone who fears Him and does what is right. He has sent this message to all of Israel, proclaiming the gospel of Jesus Christ, who is LORD of all. You know how God anointed Jesus of Nazareth with the Holy Spirit and with power, and how Jesus went around doing good and healing all who were oppressed by the devil. We are witnesses of all that He did; both in the land of the Jews and in Jerusalem. Yet they put Him to death by hanging Him on a tree, God raised Him up on the third day, and caused Him to be seen by the witnesses God had chosen before. We ate and drank with Him after He rose from the dead, and He commanded us to preach to the people and to testify that He is the One appointed by God to judge the living and the dead. All the prophets testified about Him, that everyone who believed in Him received forgiveness of sins through His name." While I was still speaking, the Holy Ghost fell on everyone who heard this message. All the circumcised believers who were with me were astounded that the Holy Ghost had been poured out on the Gentiles; for they heard them speaking in tongues and exalting God. Then I said, "Can anyone forbid them water to baptized? They have received the Holy Ghost just like we have!" So, I commanded them to be baptized in the name of Jesus Christ.

During the Feast of Unleavened Bread; I was arrested by some of Herod's guards and thrown into prison. I was guarded by four squads of four soldiers each, and Herod intended to bring me out to the people after the Passover. In the middle of the night, while I was sleeping between two soldiers, being bound with two chains, with sentries standing guard at the entrance to the prison, an angel of the LORD appeared and hit me on the side. In a daze, I woke up. I thought I was having a vision. The angel said, "Get up quickly", and the chains fell off my wrists. "Get dressed and put on your sandals," he said. I did as I was told and the angel continued to say, "Wrap your cloak around you and follow me." I followed him out, but I wasn't sure if what the angel was doing was real or a vision. We passed the first and second guards and arrived at the iron gate leading to the city. Now I'm thinking to myself, this is definitely a vision, because the gate opened by itself. We made it outside the gate and walked about one block, when the angel suddenly vanished. The chill in the night air made me realize this was really happening. I said, "Now I know for sure that the LORD has sent His angel and rescued me from Herod's prison, and from what the people were expecting." I went to the house of Mary the mother of Mark. A large group of people had gathered together and were praying. I knocked at the outer gate, and a servant girl came to see who was knocking. When she asked who it was, I responded "It is Peter" I recognized her voice as she ran off yelling "He's here, Peter is at the gate!" I called out to her, "Rhoda! Come back; open the gate." Apparently, she didn't hear me. Not sure if I was nervous or frustrated, or perhaps a little of both. I continued to knock on the gate. The last thing I wanted to do; was to be spotted by someone that would turn me back over to Herod. Finally, someone opened the door and they were shocked to see me standing there. I motioned with my hand for silence. Then I described how the LORD had brought me out of the prison. Then I said, "Send word to James and to the brothers of my escape", and then I left.

As time passed and more gentiles were baptized in the name of the LORD Jesus, and received the gift of the Holy Ghost, a group of Jewish brothers believed that the gentiles had to circumcised. The debate soon raged out of control and some brothers even took it upon themselves to command a group of gentiles to be circumcised, and to obey the law which God had given to Moses. I called a meeting of all the apostles and elders to discuss this matter before things got worse than what they already were. After everyone had an opportunity to voice their opinion, I stood up and said, "Brothers, you know God made a choice among us that the Gentiles would hear the gospel from me, and believe. God knowing every man's heart, showed His approval by giving them the Holy Ghost, just like He did to us. He made no distinction between them and us, and He cleansed their hearts by faith. So, why do you test God by placing on them a burden that neither we, nor our fathers have been able to handle? We believe; however, it is through the grace of the LORD Jesus that we are saved, just as they are." Then the entire audience grew deathly silent as Paul and Barnabas described the signs and wonders God had done among the Gentiles through them. When all was said and done, we agreed that the Gentiles should abstain from food offered to idols, from sexual immorality, from the meat of strangled animals, and from blood.

I've learned a great deal in life and have grown in the knowledge of God immensely. This one thing above all else has benefitted me the most, and I'm passing it on to you. Make every effort to add to your faith virtue; knowledge; self-control; perseverance; godliness; brotherly kindness, and love. If you have these qualities, and continue to grow in them; they will help you to be productive and effective in your knowledge of our LORD Jesus Christ. Anyone that lacks these traits has lost sight of the fact that they have been cleansed from past sins. I implore all of you: be diligent to make your calling and election sure. If you practice these things you will never stumble. I have left you letters to remind you of these things, even though you already know them and you are rooted in the truth you have received. My confidence in this message comes from being an eyewitness to the things that I am writing to you. It's not from some cleverly devised story. I was with Him when a voice from Heaven proclaimed, "This is my beloved Son, in whom I am well pleased." We also have the words of the prophets as confirmation. You would be wise to hold fast to these things because they are as important as a light to a dark path. It's also important that you understand;

no prophecy of scripture comes from anyone's private interpretation. The prophecy did not come from the intuition of man. It came from holy men of God that spoke, as they were moved by the Holy Spirit.

Now there is one last thing that I must bring to your remembrance. Humility and repentance are the key to living for God. I know you're thinking to yourself, I already know that, and that may be true. However, knowing it, and applying it are totally different things. Humility allows you to admit your mistakes or wrong doings so they can be dealt with. You must not allow your pride to hinder you from seeking help. Repentance, allows Jesus to cover you with His mercy, and to cleanse you with His blood. There are no greater contrasts of how to, or not to deal with your failure, or your most embarrassing moment, than myself and Judas. Judas, after he betrayed Jesus, went back to the high priest and repented. Problem with that was, the high priest helped get him into this situation, and was therefore incapable of doing anything to help Judas with his sin problem. Judas then added insult to injury and hung himself, ensuring that Jesus couldn't help him with his sin problem. I on the other hand, after denying Jesus, wept bitterly, and repented to Jesus upon seeing Him after His resurrection. He then forgave me, and commissioned and equipped me to tend to His then future church.

Onesimus: From Disgraced Slave to Trusted Brother

Yeah, yeah; I know most of you are thinking to yourselves who is this? Most people don't know anything about me, and the few that do, are left with a lot of speculation and perhaps even some misgivings about my life. This is my story (kind of), but it's more a story of the transformative power of the Holy Ghost. You see, not much is known of my life. In fact, if it weren't for a single-page letter from Bro. Paul, you probably wouldn't even know I existed.

I was a slave to a man named Philemon, and as you will soon discover I was a thief. Philemon was a wealthy man and a minister at Colossae. Being a christian man, he was not like most slave masters. He was a decent and fair man; life as a slave in his house was not miserable. One day, I stole something from him and ran away in fear for my life. I ended up in Rome and was constantly looking over my shoulder. You see the penalty for theft at that time was death, so I was no safer in Rome than I was in Colossae. I'm almost certain my master reported my thievery to the authorities, so I had to be extremely cautious everywhere I went. Hence, little is known about me other than I'm a disgraced thief and runaway slave.

Then, there was my chance meeting with the apostle Paul. How I met him is a source of speculation, even today. Was I a prisoner, like him, or was I just a worker in the prison? The whys and wherefores are not the important part. The important part is how my encounter with Paul, change my life FOREVER! Paul witnessed to me. He explained to me the love of God and the power of the Holy Ghost. I surrendered my life to Jesus and was baptized. I received the Holy Ghost and fellowshipped with Paul and Timothy often. I ministered to Paul while he was in prison and he helped me understand God's love and my purpose in life. Our relationship became so strong that I became a valuable asset to Paul and his ministry.

Now the time has come for me to return to Colossae, and reconcile with my master. I returned with a letter from Bro. Paul to Philemon. This letter is the most profound demonstration of the power of forgiveness and reconciliation ever written. It reads as follows:

I'm happy and encouraged by your love because you have renewed the hearts of the saints. Although, in Christ, I am bold enough to demand that you do what is proper. I prefer to appeal to you based on love. I appeal to you for my son Onesimus, whose father I became while I was in prison. Before now, he was not useful to you, but now he has become useful to me and hopefully to you. I am sending him back to you as one who is dear to my heart. I would have loved to keep him with me so that he could continue to minister to me in my chains for the gospel. However, I did not want to do anything without your consent. So, your kindness will not be out of obligation, but by your own free will. Perhaps this is why he was separated from you for a while. So that you might have him back for good; no longer as a slave, but as a beloved brother. He is especially beloved to me, but even more so to you, both in person and in the Lord. So, if you consider me a partner, receive him as you would receive me. If he has wronged you in any way or owes you anything; charge it to my account. I'm writing this with my hand. I will repay it; not saying that you owe me your very self. Yes brother, let me have some joy from you in the Lord. Renew my heart in Christ. I'm confident of your obedience, knowing that you will do even more than I ask. In the meantime, prepare a guest room for me, because I hope that through your prayers, I will be restored to you. The grace of the Lord Jesus Christ be with your spirit.

After reading the letter, Philemon forgave me of my sin against his house, and welcomed me, not as a slave, but as a brother. After that, I ministered with him in Colossae until my death.

Bibliography

Scofield, C.I., The Scofield Study Bible. New York: Oxford University Press Inc., 2003.